WILD FLOWERS *of the* NORTH HIGHLANDS *of* SCOTLAND

Wild Flowers
of the North Highlands
of Scotland

KEN BUTLER

Photographs by
KEN CROSSAN

BIRLINN | 2009

First published in 2009 by
Birlinn Limited
West Newington House
10 Newington Road
Edinburgh
EH9 1QS

www.birlinn.co.uk

ISBN: 978 1 84158 832 2

British Library Cataloguing-in-Publication Data
A catalogue record for this book is available from the British Library

The Publisher acknowledges the generous support of the
North Highland Initiative towards the publication of this book

Designed by Mark Blackadder
Typeset by Davidson Publishing Solutions, Glasgow
Printed and bound by Bell &Bain Ltd, Glasgow

Contents

Foreword

The North Highlands has a magnificent range of natural assets, many of which are rather under-appreciated. Over the years, since childhood, I have been lucky enough to visit some of the area and, as a result, to develop an awareness of its immensely rich natural heritage. I hope that the many special features about the nature, history and culture of the North Highlands will become more widely appreciated because out of this splendid environment comes a fascinating history, high quality local produce and a way of living that in many respects is in harmony with the natural surroundings. In similar vein, my Grandmother, Queen Elizabeth The Queen Mother, had an abiding love of the area and spent almost fifty happy Summers at the Castle of Mey, from where she enjoyed the scenic coast, the grandeur of the mountains in the West and the multitude of rivers and lochs. She also became very fond of immersing herself in the culture of the area.

This book has been created by two people who understand that the wild plants of the North Highlands have a rather unique quality of their own and deserve to be explained and interpreted for the benefit of the resident and the visitor. The beauty of the detail in many of the plants is quite remarkable and I was delighted to see it has been so well portrayed. It seems to me that there is a real significance in observing and describing not only the plants themselves, but also the way in which they form a habitat, for it is by understanding the various habitats that we will be able to conserve and avoid damaging them. I do hope that the reader will enjoy learning about the importance of the flora through this book, which helps to shed light on a less obvious, but nonetheless spectacular element of the very special landscape of the North Highlands…

Chapter 1. Introduction

Wild flowers are beautiful and their variety, colour and form appeal to our sense of wonder. The North Highlands of Scotland is an exquisite area on the edge of the Atlantic Ocean. We bring the plants and the area together, knowing that it is a combination which is inspiring, interesting and well worthy of exploration and enjoyment.

The purpose of this book is to introduce a selection of the common plants of the North Highlands that the resident and the visitor would want to know about, plus some plants that inhabit the more interesting places, and also a few whose rarity makes them worthy of attention. The visitor can use this book to discover something of the delights of the area while the resident might use it as a starting point for deeper exploration.

We also hope to show that most plants possess a singular beauty, sometimes in their stature and proportions, and often in the close-up detail of their structure. Ken Crossan's photographs purposefully seek out this beauty and perhaps might even bring the reader, quite literally, to his or her knees in admiration of the plants.

Beyond the mere recognition of species there lies a deeper world of ecology, whereby an understanding develops of the relationship between a species and its habitat. Why a species lives where it does and the way it has adapted to survive and prosper in that habitat is something that the curious mind can explore for a lifetime. The North Highlands is a good place to see these ecological relationships at work because the climate, topography and geology are varied and often extreme.

These things can be explored in a landscape which is breathtaking in its splendour. It is a rewarding experience to stand alone in an open peatland, with no other human in sight, and see the plants and birds that have learned to survive in this wet and unforgiving environment. To stand on a headland looking across to islands in the Atlantic Ocean and to have at one's feet the tiny plants that thrive in the salty gales and on thin stony soil, leads one to wonder at the determination of nature to adapt to every natural circumstance.

Bog Cranberry

Water Forget-me-not

Corn Marigold

Creeping Willow

Cross-leaved Heath

Melancholy Thistle

Pyramidal Bugle

Scottish Primrose

Fragrant cherry

Cloudberry

The area described is the northernmost part of the Scottish mainland, comprising the counties of Sutherland and Caithness and part of Easter Ross. There is a larger-scale map in Chapter 7 on page 165.

The book is arranged around five types of vegetation, with each species described in one of its common habitats. Chapter 7 sets the context for the plants and habitats by giving some detail concerning the geology, environmental history and climate. It would be logical to put this at the beginning of the book but our eagerness to show off our wonderful plants overcame this sense of tidiness; some may wish to read it early in their exploration of the book. The locations of places named in the text are often given as Ordnance Survey map references and the use of these is also explained in detail in Chapter 7.

Location of our area within the United Kingdom

Chapter 2. The Sea Coast

Oldshoremore Bay in West Sutherland

The North Highlands has a truly spectacular and fascinating coastline and it is one of the prime attractions of the area for scenery, birds and plant-life. Some of the highest cliffs in Britain are located here, and some of the most exposed to Atlantic storms. Beaches are often at the head of a bay, with a dune system behind them due to high winds piling up the beach sand. Beyond the dunes there will be the dune links – a substantial area of ground which has been affected by blown sand and has a sandy well-drained soil with its own particular vegetation. There are low rocky shores where the action of the waves sweeps away the sand and only leaves in place the eroded base rocks and boulders. On the sea coast the plants have to be sufficiently tolerant of salt and able to survive the harsh weather. In addition to the common sea-coast plants of Europe, some of the plants to be found are particular to northern latitudes, giving us a link to Scandinavia and Iceland. There is another group of specialities, the plants left behind from the last ice age, surviving here because the climate is still suitable and because they never were overwhelmed by the more aggressive

Sea Pink in its form when growing in a rock crevice

Sea Mayweed growing on bare sand

common plants that populated Britain when the climate warmed up.

COMMON PLANTS OF THE COAST

The **Sea Pink** (*Armeria maritima*) is common all round the coast of Britain. Its hemispherical head of flowers appears in the early summer above a rosette of needle-like leaves. On the rocky shore and the vertical cliffs it will inhabit cracks in the rock and resist all attempts of the waves to dislodge it. It is also very tolerant of salt, so it ventures well down the tide-line and is one of the lowest-level inhabitants of the rocky shore. On clifftop turf it becomes luxuriant, expanding into big hummocks, especially if the soil is enriched by the droppings of nesting or roosting birds.

The **Sea Mayweed** (*Tripleurospermum maritimum*) is also common round the sea coast of Britain. It has bold, white, daisy-like flower heads and much-divided leaves. Like the Sea Pink it is a truly maritime plant with a high tolerance of

Scurvygrass; the leaf shape indicates *Cochlearia officinalis*

seawater and an ability to live in several shoreline substrates. It is at home in the cracks in vertical cliff-faces where it has an upright stance. It lives in sand at the strand-line, where it adopts a rather floppy and spreading habit, and also in the marginal grass and amongst the rocks of the upper shoreline.

Scurvygrass (*Cochlearia officinalis* agg.) is the common name of a group of species which are particularly complex in northern Scotland and botanists have not yet resolved the naming of some of them. Thick, succulent, bright green leaves are topped with small, usually white, flowers bearing four petals. The leaves are edible and they contain a good amount of vitamin C. Hence the name: sailors of old, who were prone to the condition called 'scurvy' brought on by a shortage of vitamin C, used to eat the leaves of the Scurvygrass widely available by the sea.

Scurvygrass can be found in rock crevices quite low in the tidal zone and

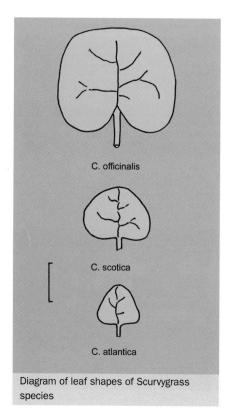

C. officinalis

C. scotica

C. atlantica

Diagram of leaf shapes of Scurvygrass species

Sea Rocket in its typical habitat

Sea Sandwort

topped by four-petalled flowers of mauve or pink. It is worth bending to catch the rich, sweet perfume that it imparts.

Sea Sandwort (*Honckenya peploides*) has flowers with five narrow, greenish-white petals and thick, succulent green leaves and lies procumbent on the beach above the strand-line. It is very common where there is sand; it has extensive underground stems and roots that fix it even on a stormy beach and it has a good tolerance of salt.

Kidney Vetch (*Anthyllis vulneraria*) as its name suggests, is a member of the pea family of plants and has its pea-like yellow flowers in a spherical head. The leaves are compound – each leaf consists of (usually) seven leaflets. There are two obviously different subspecies in our area.

well up the shore. It is one of the plants to look for along the banks of a river as an indicator of how far up-river the tidal influence of the sea is carried. It will also grow in clifftop turf and on the gravelly surface of a harbour or coastal road.

In our area look out for the common form of Scurvygrass with large circular leaves of around 3 cm diameter which are part of a plant some 15 cm high. Also see the smaller Scottish Scurvygrass with leaves only 1 cm diameter and flattened at the base. And in the far north-west look amongst the clifftop turf for the even smaller Atlantic Scurvygrass.

Sea Rocket (*Cakile maritima*) is a real gem of a plant on a sandy shore. It is very tolerant of seawater and occupies the upper strand-line area of a beach. Its thick, succulent, light green leaves are

- *Anthyllis vulneraria* subsp. *vulneraria* is the least common. It has lemon-yellow flowers with hardly noticeable red tips to the calyx lobes and leaves with the terminal leaflet about the same size as the others
- *Anthyllis vulneraria* subsp. *lapponica* is more common in our area. It has flowers of a darker yellow and noticeable red colouration of the calyx.

Kidney Vetch with leaflets clasping the stem

Sea Spleenwort in crevices of Old Red sandstone

THE SEA CLIFFS

The sea cliffs of the North Highlands are spectacular. The Old Red sandstone cliffs of Caithness, the white limestone cliffs of Durness and Whiten Head and the great Lewisian gneiss cliffs of Cape Wrath are examples of the variety of rock types and locations involved. One thing they have in common is that they are shaped by the waves and lashing stormy rain. There are but a few plants that are content to live in such a place so the cliffs mostly look bare. There are specialised lichens and mosses that colonise the bare rock but flowering plants need a crevice or a sheltered ledge to get established. In general the Old Red sandstone provides good cracks and fissures, Durness limestone provides ledges and Lewisian gneiss is rather lacking in either.

Areas where birds nest can provide a source of plant life. Birds produce guano which is high in nitrogen and promotes a lush growth of 'farmyard weeds' on any big ledges that are sufficiently sheltered. Another type of lush growth can occur where the cliff has been eroded or faulted into a narrow bay or 'geo'. Geo (pronounced with a hard 'g') is an

The leaves have a terminal leaflet much larger than the lateral leaflets. This subspecies has a northerly distribution in Britain, extending through Fennoscandia and north Russia

Kidney Vetch is found well above high tide and ventures into the vegetation above the shore such as stable sand dunes, clifftop turf, rock crevices and links turf. In some parts of our area it is the principal food of the Little Blue butterfly which is scarce in Britain.

When very young the basal leaflets clasp the stem, a habit deeply engrained in the pea family.

Old Norse word for a special type of narrow, parallel-sided inlet, usually arising because there are two parallel fault lines perpendicular to the cliff and the rock between the faults has slipped or eroded away. Smoo Cave is at the head of a limestone geo, and there is a good seabird colony at Duncansby in the Geo of Sclaites.

Common sea-coast plants to be seen on the cliffs are Sea Pink, Sea Mayweed and Scurvygrass.

The **Sea Spleenwort** (*Asplenium marinum*) is a fern which specialises in occupying horizontal crevices just above the tide-line on otherwise bare cliff-faces, though it does also move into the more sheltered bays and geos; it is found on the coast throughout our area. Sea Spleenwort is easily recognised since it is the only fern in such a habitat. Its fronds are less than 10 cm long and glossy green with thick, leathery frond lobes.

Roseroot (*Sedum rosea*) belongs to a family of succulents and this species is well adapted to exposed places since it occurs on alpine cliffs in Europe as well as on the seashore in our area. It has yellow flowers in a terminal domed head and many thick grey-green leaves

Old Red sandstone cliffs weathered and shaped by the sea at Duncansby Head, Caithness

Roseroot in a crevice of Old Red sandstone

Scots Lovage on clifftop grass

arranged on the stalk. We find it on cliffs that have a bit of shelter and have some calcium dissolved in the groundwater that oozes from the rock fissures, so ideal spots are rock ledges and the bigger fissures in the geos and bays. The plant is frequent especially in the west.

Scots Lovage (*Ligusticum scoticum*) is another component of the cliff flora, occupying sheltered grassy ledges on the cliffs or sometimes the grassy zone at the top of a cliff. It may be recognised by its mid-green, leathery, toothed leaves and its umbel of green-and-white-petalled flowers. It occurs around the whole coast of Scotland and is quite frequent in our area. It was commonly used as a strong-tasting pot herb in stews and during hard times the roots were chewed if tobacco was not available.

ROCKY SHORES, ESTUARIES AND GRASSY HINTERLAND

If we think of cliffs as big vertical walls, rocky shores are close to their horizontal equivalent. Here the rock was shaped by the previous action of glaciation thousands of years ago and is now broken up by the waves. This is usually a place where the wave action is too severe to allow sand to linger, thus the lower shore is limited to plants that can withstand severe conditions and further up the shore there are crevices, ledges and gaps between boulders that provide plant habitats.

This is the main home of the Sea Pink, the Sea Mayweed, the Scurvygrass and the Kidney Vetch.

The **Sea Plantain** (*Plantago maritima*) is a small plant with a recognisable rosette

A rocky shoreline; the waves have eroded the rock to show the layers of sediment

of simple leaves and with its small and dull flowers easily passed over. It is common all around Britain's shores.

Sea Campion (*Silene uniflora*) is also a common plant of the seashore which is usually to be found amongst the upper shore rocks. It has a white flower with a prominent calyx below it, which arises from prostrate blue-green stems and leaves.

Rather more special is the **Oyster Plant** (*Mertensia maritima*) which is scarce and declining in Britain, being confined to the east and north coasts of Scotland. Perhaps disturbance is the cause of its decline due to the increasing use of seashores for people's recreation. It can appear as an annual or biennial plant amongst rocks and sand on the upper shore, each plant having a few lateral shoots bearing beautiful blue-green leaves and flowers that are deep blue with a tendency to pink. Further up the shore, where there is less disturbance from winter storms, there can be larger, established perennial plants growing as prostrate stems to even a metre diameter

Sea Plantain

Sea Campion showing flowers, bud and capsules

Oyster Plant high on a beach. It is sometimes found on a boulder beach

forms mats of white flowers with pink-backed petals. The thick swollen leaves also have a pink tinge.

Where the waters are sheltered, and at slow-flowing river estuaries, the shore can be muddy. The plants that grow on the mud form a close turf which binds the mud to make a stable growth platform

Sea Milkwort

which survive for many years. Sadly these bigger established plants become fewer every year. The flowers, leaves and roots are edible and the thick fleshy leaves are said to taste strongly of oyster. One might look for it in our area at Dunbeath on the east coast and to the west of Castletown on the north coast.

At the upper shoreline and amongst the short turf above the shore one often finds the **Sea Milkwort** (*Glaux maritima*). It is also frequent in the short turf at the top of sea cliffs and in the salt-marsh turf of muddy places. The leafy stems have pale pink flowers in the axils of the leaves. It is quite unlike a true Milkwort and you might wonder at the value of such a misleading name!

Among the rocks on the west coast the **English Stonecrop** (*Sedum anglicum*)

English Stonecrop on a bed of Woolly Fringe-moss

Sea Aster

known as a salt marsh. There are large areas of salt marsh on the east coast by the Cromarty Firth and Dornoch Firth, and on the north coast at the Kyle of Tongue and Loch Eriboll. The west coast, with its many sheltered waters might be expected to have a lot of salt marsh, but in fact the glacial scouring of the inlets left them with many steep-sided shores unsuitable for mud accumulation at the shoreline, so the salt marsh is usually a smaller area at the head of the inlet. The turf is mainly composed of specialist maritime grasses of the genus *Puccinellia*, amongst which there are some common seashore plants such as Sea Pink, Sea Plantain, Scurvygrass and Sea Milkwort along with some maritime sedges and rushes.

The **Sea Aster** (*Aster tripolium*) is also a prominent member of this community and it is the only habitat in which Sea Aster appears in quantity, though it does occur in small numbers in rock crevices and cliff ledges. It is a blue-flowered, daisy-like plant.

An attractive flower of this habitat is the **Greater Sea-spurrey** (*Spergularia media*) with violet flowers and awl-shaped leaves. It sprawls over the mud, forming patches.

Greater Sea-spurrey

The beautiful and scarce Seaside Centaury

On the east coast around the Kyle of Sutherland, the Dornoch Firth and the Morrich More there are good colonies of the **Seaside Centaury** (*Centaurium* *littorale*) which is a scarce plant around Britain. It inhabits the upper salt marsh and has pink flowers on a stem up to 10 cm tall with narrow leaves. It is a plant of great beauty and well worth the trouble to go and find it.

Where the mud occurs in a river estuary the water (and the mud) will be brackish due to dilution with river water – and this is so for the extent up-river of the tidal influence. One of the special plants of our area, the **Estuarine Sedge** (*Carex recta*) is established in this habitat and is to be found in three sites: the Wick River, the Beauly River and the Kyle of Sutherland. These are the only sites in Britain and there are only a few more in the wider world, all on the eastern seaboard of North America. The plant was first found in the Wick River in 1885 by local botanist J. Grant so it is known locally as the 'Wick Sedge'. Estuarine Sedge reaches about 1 m high in dense stands in the margins of the rivers in the tidal zone. It is similar to the **Water Sedge** (*Carex aquatilis*); the main difference is that the flower spikes of Estuarine Sedge have glumes (scales that cover the fruit) with elongated points, while Water Sedge has only small blunt points. The difference is shown in the adjacent diagram including an illustration of the intermediate state of the hybrid between them, *Carex* x *grantii* (the name commemorates J. Grant). Estuarine Sedge can be seen on the Wick River at ND350515 and thereabouts, and below Carbisdale Castle on the Kyle of Sutherland at NH576954.

The flowering head of the Estuarine Sedge

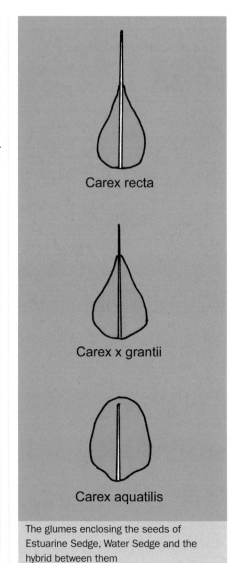

Carex recta

Carex x grantii

Carex aquatilis

The glumes enclosing the seeds of Estuarine Sedge, Water Sedge and the hybrid between them

The rocky shore and the clifftop merge with the adjacent vegetation in a transformation zone. This is a zone where the salt-laden winds carry the influence of the sea inland, and in the strong winds and stormy seas of north Scotland that influence is usually noticeable for around 5 km inland of the sea. What actually grows in this zone depends on the type of soil and vegetation that is present: if there is deep mineral soil then there can be a mass of tall herbs; if the soil is thin mineral soil it will be short grass; where the soil is peaty it develops a maritime heath.

The tall herb community along the shoreline used to be cut down by grazing animals, but in recent years it has become more obvious because of fencing which excludes grazing close to the shore. The hinterland is most often farmland and this type of vegetation is common in the east half of our area, especially in Caithness. It is dominated by Hogweed, Bracken, Thistles and tall tussocky grasses, with frequent invasion by Gorse.

On thinner mineral soil the grassy sward is short, with **Red Fescue** (*Festuca rubra*) the dominant fine grass. Sea Pink can form big tussocks especially if seabirds roost. Sea Milkwort is common in the

Tall herbs on a shore of deep mineral soil. The plants are around 1 m high

Eyebright. This is *Euphrasia arctica* subsp. *borealis*

Scottish Primrose in dune-links turf

grass, as is Kidney Vetch. This is the preferred home of the **Eyebright** (*Euphrasia* species). The north coast is a Mecca for different Eyebright species but the botany is complex and not well understood, so we will not delve too deeply here. The common Eyebright of this habitat is *Euphrasia arctica* subsp. *borealis* which has white flowers tinged with violet and small toothed leaves which are leathery and shiny. Reay golf course in Caithness has the best show of this plant but it is not uncommon throughout our area.

The short, fine, coastal grassland is also the main home of the **Scottish Primrose** (*Primula scotica*). This beautiful miniature primrose with deep-pink flowers is 5 cm high with flowers up to 1 cm diameter. It grows only in Sutherland, Caithness and Orkney – its world distribution. It has a basal rosette of leaves very similar to those of the common Daisy, but with a paler surface that seems to be sprinkled with flour (i.e. it is farinose). The leaf rosettes of barren plants are often easier to find than those of flowering plants.

It grows in the shortest turf on clifftops and in sandy turf on dune links, usually in substantial colonies of a hundred or so plants.

Scottish Primrose is related to the Birdseye Primrose (*Primula farinosa*) of the north Pennines and to *Primula norvegica* in Norway, but has developed, in isolation since the end of the last ice age, enough individual characters to be regarded as a separate species. There are many sites where it might be seen along the north coast of our area and the easiest

Spring Squill

A sandy shore at Brora beach

are Strathy Point (near the lighthouse) and Dunnet Links where the Highland Ranger Service usually knows of a good flowering site. Flowering occurs from April to June, with a second flowering in August. Some rosettes will flower twice so they will have ripening seed and fresh flowers on the same plant.

Another pretty plant of this habitat is the **Spring Squill** (*Scilla verna*) which can be found in clifftop turf along the north coast. It is a bulbous plant and can use its stored food to come into flower in April when the clifftops are still cold and the grass is not growing. It has blue star-like flowers on a stalk only 3 cm high. Its distinctive seed capsule is easy to recognise throughout the summer.

SANDY SHORES

Over most of our coast the sea is too stormy and the tidal currents too strong to permit sand to settle on the shore. The exception is around Brora, Golspie and Dornoch on the east coast where there are fairly long lengths of coastal strand. Otherwise the sandy beaches are

An Orache on a pebble beach. This one is *Atriplex laciniata*

Marram Grass. Note the small, thin flower heads

Lyme Grass. Note the robust flower heads

confined to bays and inlets where the currents are less strong and the sand cannot be carried away. These can be quite large beaches, especially Achnahaird Bay, Sandwood Bay, Balnakeil Bay, Dunnet Bay, Sinclair Bay and Morrich More. The type of sand varies. When it is local rock finely ground, it only stays on the beach if it is within a certain size range – when it has been ground too fine the sea sweeps it away to deeper water. Lime-rich sand can often be ground-up seashells. It is usually a mixture of the two.

Sandy beaches have a rather sparse population of highly specialised plants, because the sand is very salty, unstable and exposed. Sea Rocket and Sea Sandwort are the two common residents and in rare cases the Oyster Plant might be found near the top of the beach.

Another very common plant is the **Orache** (*Atriplex* species) which builds up over the summer and flowers in late August with fruits maturing in September. You could be forgiven for not recognising the flowers of Orache since they look like two tiny leaves placed back to back. There are four species in our area but they are tricky to differentiate. They all produce black seeds which are able to spread via the sea or by the winter turmoil on the beach.

Onshore winds pick up the sand from the beach and carry it inland. Most winds only carry the relatively heavy particles a short distance, maybe 200 m. There the sand piles up to form sand dunes which are typically 30 m high. Historically the dunes have been unstable, with later winds carrying the sand from the peaks further inland and particularly severe storms disrupting the dune shape with blowouts. All dunes in our area naturally have, or have been planted with, **Marram Grass** (*Ammophila arenaria*) to stabilise the sand so that the roads and farms behind the dunes are protected from being overwhelmed by sand during a storm. Marram is good at its job: long roots (they can be 10 m long) permeate the sand and bind it together; stout stems around 1 m high stand against the wind and slow it down over the surface of the sand; leaves with waxy outer surfaces can curl up to a cylinder to restrict water loss and allow the plant to survive periods without water in this free-draining medium.

The seaward edge of the dunes is just above high tide and relatively undisturbed. The salt levels are high and the dune front sometimes collapses onto it. The most common plant is **Lyme Grass** (*Leymus arenarius*) which is taller than Marram and of a lighter green – a very handsome grass.

Also at the dune front one frequently finds **Corn Sow-thistle** (*Sonchus arvensis*) with its yellow thistle-like flower on a tall stem more than 1 m high. It has been

Corn Sow-thistle

Hogweed. Note the large palmate leaves

called a Milk-thistle, because if the stem is broken it exudes a white milky substance. It is late flowering – a harbinger of autumn. In addition to its liking for foreshores it is frequently found in roadside verges where it might typically form a group of 20 plants.

The peaks of the dunes are dry, salty and unstable and do not find favour with many plants. Three umbelliferous plants find a home here. **Hogweed** (*Heracleum sphondylium*) is over a metre high with large coarse leaves and a flat umbel of white flowers. It is also a common plant of grassland and clifftops in the east, but less common in the west. **Wild Angelica** (*Angelica sylvestris*) is shorter and stouter with a hemispherical umbel of grey-white flowers and leaves which are green, toothed and somewhat leathery. It is also common in marshy habitats and clifftop grassland. The **Wild Carrot** (*Daucus carota*) is shorter still, typically 15 cm high, with a dense umbel of white flowers and finely divided leaves. It is special to the sand dunes of the west.

A notably tall and coarse plant of the unstable sandy places is **Lesser Burdock** (*Arctium minus*). The leaves are large, oval and dark green. The flowers are thistle-like heads, not spiny but with hooks on the bracts at the base of the flower head so that the flower in seed can stick to animal coats and be carried to a new site.

With a yellow flower, but a very small and fine one, is **Lady's Bedstraw** (*Galium verum*). All bedstraws have their leaves in whorls around the stem and this is the only one here with yellow flowers – the rest are white-flowered. Lady's Bedstraw can be found in the sand dunes and on the dune-links turf. It does not like too much competition, so dies out where the turf is denser. In the Middle Ages it was used to stuff mattresses because of its springy texture and its pleasant smell. It was also used to curdle the milk in cheese-making.

Wild Angelica. The domed flower heads and stout stems are recognisable

Wild Carrot is small and delicate with dissected bracts below the flower head

Lesser Burdock in sand-dune habitat

Lady's Bedstraw

Delicate turf forms behind the dunes

DUNE LINKS AND MACHAIR

Behind the sand dunes is flat ground formed by the finer grade of sand that has been blown over the dunes to cover the base rock during the thousands of years since the last ice age. The sand is stable and it has developed a thin layer of humus (the decayed remains of plants which adds fertility). It takes a few hundred years to form the stable humus layer, so the habitat is very fragile and easily destroyed. On this humus layer grows a sward of fine grasses and small plants. This dune links area might be 2 km across perpendicular to the shore given the ability of strong winds to carry the sand inland. It makes the best golf courses, as evidenced by Tain, Dornoch, Brora, Reiss, Durness and Reay course locations.

A dune slack, dominated by Bogbean and Marsh Marigold

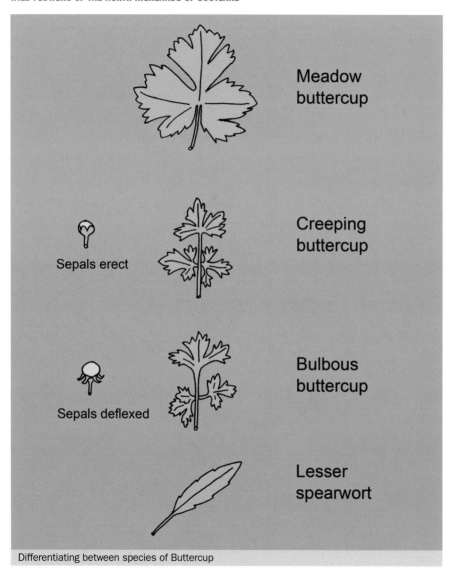

Sepals erect

Sepals deflexed

Meadow buttercup

Creeping buttercup

Bulbous buttercup

Lesser spearwort

Differentiating between species of Buttercup

Machair is a term applied to this type of ground in the west of Scotland, and especially in the Western Isles, where a particular type of grazing and arable agriculture has given the habitat a range of plants and an appearance which is unique and rare in world terms. The dune links of our area is similar to machair and has a lot of plant species in common. There is not the same rotation of ground into arable and then grazing as in the Western Isles since here this type of ground is mostly used for permanent grazing of sheep and cattle and hence has a more settled long-term population of species which, in the best examples, makes it more diverse. Authors writing about machair vegetation vary in opinion as to whether our dune links should be called machair or not.

The best places for good quality vegetation of this type are Sandwood Bay, Durness, Invernaver, Strathy East, Dunnet and Greenland Links, Keiss Links, Dornoch Links and Morrich More.

Although sandy loam is inherently free-draining, water can lie in a rock basin or a clay basin below the sand. This creates dry habitats and wet 'dune slack' habitats which are quite different in their vegetation.

First we should introduce some species which characterise the dune-link habitat. It is a grassy habitat and the most frequent grasses are Red Fescue, Yorkshire Fog (*Holcus lanatus*), and Spreading Meadow-grass (*Poa humilis*). Buttercups abound: in the drier parts the **Bulbous Buttercup** (*Ranunculus bulbosus*) whose sepals droop down; in the moderately moist places the **Creeping Buttercup** (*Ranunculus repens*) and **Meadow Buttercup** (*Ranunculus acris*); then in the wettest places the **Lesser Spearwort** (*Ranunculus flammula*) with its spear-shaped leaves quite distinct from those of the other species. The diagram on page 36 may help to differentiate the Buttercups.

The **Birdsfoot Trefoil** (*Lotus corniculatus*) has moderately-sized pea-type yellow flowers and leaves of three leaflets. Another common trefoil in this habitat is the **White Clover** (*Trifolium repens*) with its spherical head of white flowers, which creeps over the ground and can live in very poor mineral soil.

Where calcareous groundwater flushes to the surface the **Grass of Parnassus** (*Parnassia palustris*) is often found. It is a beautiful plant: from a basal rosette of leaves arises a single stem with one

Birdsfoot Trefoil

White Clover flower head

Flowers and buds of Grass of Parnassus

Marsh-orchid (*Dactylorhiza purpurella*) whose flat, dark-purple flower-lip and broad (usually unspotted but sometimes spotted) leaves are characteristic. It prefers damp grassland whether sandy or not, being just as successful on clay. It will stray onto peat moor but prefers mineral soil.

In addition to the normal form there is, mostly on the north and east coast from Melvich to Dunbeath, a different form of Northern Marsh-orchid which has strongly spotted leaves and a flower with a lighter purple base colour in which the loops and dots on the flower-lip are more prominent. This is *Dactylorhiza purpurella* var. *cambrensis* which is rare in Britain, occurring in our area and in a few places in Ireland and in Wales.

Northern Marsh-orchid with Heath Speedwell

The scarce *Dactylorhiza purpurella* var. *cambrensis* has not yet been given an English name

prominent leaf. Above it is a single flower of five white petals, which has five yellow stamens interspersed with many tiny yellow staminodes. It flowers from July to September and is common in flushed sites in dune-links turf, as well as other places in grasslands where there is flushed calcareous water.

Almost all the orchids of our area occur on the dune-links habitat, so it is useful to mention them here.

One common orchid is the **Northern**

The Heath Spotted-orchid is common on peaty ground

A second common orchid is the **Heath Spotted-orchid** (*Dactylorhiza maculata*) which has a pale-purple flower-lip and narrow spotted leaves. The flower colour may vary to almost white. Note that the small tongue at the bottom of the flower-lip is shorter than the bottom margin. It is confined to acid, peaty habitats where it can occur in great numbers. It is a common sight in July on a peat moor.

The Northern Marsh-orchid and the Heath Spotted-orchid sometimes hybridise when they are in the same locality, so you may spot them with obvious intermediate characters.

Another less common member of the *Dactylorhiza* family is the **Early Marsh-orchid** (*Dactylorhiza incarnata*). In its classic form it has paler green leaves than the Northern Marsh-orchid and they are distinctly hooded at the tip. Its flower is

flesh pink to brick red but can be very pale or almost white. The flower-lip is strongly curved back so the flower looks long and narrow. This is the form that is found on the damper ground of dune links.

Early Marsh-orchid. This is a pale form of subsp. *pulchella*

The other form of Early Marsh-orchid that is in our area is *Dactylorhiza incarnata* subsp. *pulchella* which looks like the one above, except that the flower colour is purplish and it inhabits wet acid habitats especially in the west of our area. It can be the dominant Purple Orchid in wet bogs on the west coast.

In a few places in Sutherland and Wester Ross the rare *Dactylorhiza incarnata* subsp. *cruenta* occurs with purplish flowers and heavily blotched and spotted leaves. Its detailed description is available in specialist books such as Foley & Clarke 2005 in our bibliography.

The **Frog Orchid** is now called *Dactylorhiza viridis*, though many know it as *Coeloglossum viride*. It is often tiny, especially on dune links where it is typically 5 cm tall. It likes a place with short grassy turf, with some minerals in the soil, so dune links are ideal, as are grassy flushes in heaths and even the peaty turf of maritime heath if the sea spray has enriched the turf with mineral salts. The flowers are green, often tinged or suffused with reddish brown. It has a very prominent flower-lip which has three lobes at the tip.

The **Early Purple Orchid** (*Orchis mascula*) is frequent in the west of our area, but scarce in the east. This has more to do with geology than with climate, for it is a plant that favours a limestone soil and the true limestone is exposed as part of the Moine Thrust from Durness southwards. However, small colonies do occur on the east and north coasts where there is suitable mineral soil.

When compared to the Northern Marsh-orchid, the Early Purple can be distinguished thus:

The Frog Orchid is usually about 5 cm tall in our area

Early Purple Orchid. Note the large lower lip of the flower

- Short, green upper leaves that are upright and clasp the stem
- Flowers whose flower-lip has no purple loops and spots but instead has a whitish central patch that includes white spots

The Fragrant Orchid. This is *Gymnadenia densiflora*, the most common species

It is a delight to sniff the **Fragrant Orchid** (*Gymnadenia densiflora*). It gives a rich clove or carnation smell. It was called *Gymnadenia conopsea* until the assessment of its DNA showed that three very distinct species were present and not being clearly distinguished because of their physical similarities. Of these three it is *Gymnadenia densiflora* and *Gymnadenia borealis* that are the most common in our area, though the newly defined *Gymnadenia conopsea* has also been recorded. There is a need to re-examine the plants in our area and get a better understanding of what we have. The differentiation of the three species is beyond the scope of this book and readers should refer to a specialist flora such as Foley & Clarke 2005.

The Fragrant Orchid has unspotted, erect, moderately broad, light-green leaves that are slightly hooded at the tip. The flowers are a strong pink and the flower spike is slim. The flower-lip is three-lobed. It is most common on dune links where it can form substantial colonies. But it also appears in mineral-rich peaty heath and in mineral-rich hill flushes.

To complete our list of orchids on the dune links we have the **Common Twayblade Orchid** (*Neottia ovata*) which many readers might know as *Listera ovata* since the change of name was recently brought about as a result of DNA evidence of its close affinity with other *Neottia* species. It gets its name from the

There are the most beautiful **Field Gentians** (*Gentianella campestris*) on the dune links in our area, flowering in late July with blue-purple flowers. These are not as large and showy as the Gentians of the Alps, but they give an impressive display when in a large group. Greenland Links on Dunnet Bay probably has the best show. They are closely related to the **Autumn Gentian** (*Gentianella amarella*) and they often grow together, the Field being larger than the Autumn. To distinguish between them it is best to examine the sepals – the green

The Common Twayblade Orchid

Field Gentian

Autumn Gentian

two large opposite leaves which are at the base of the flower stalk. The flower is yellow-green on a green (or sometimes reddish) stalk so the plant can be inconspicuous until the basal leaves are recognised. Although it is known to grow in a wide range of habitats across Britain, it is found in our area on lime-rich grassland, especially dune links.

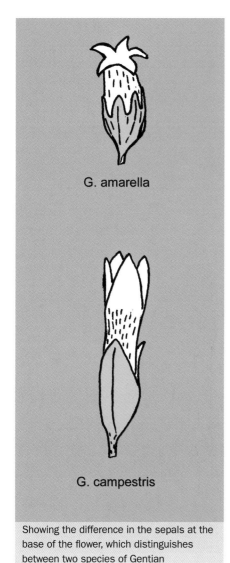

G. amarella

G. campestris

Showing the difference in the sepals at the base of the flower, which distinguishes between two species of Gentian

structures just below the petals. They are quite different in shape, as shown in the diagram. The Autumn Gentians of our area can be of the common sort with purple flowers or a scarcer sort with creamy-white flowers which is known to botanists as *Gentianella amarella* subsp. *septentrionale*.

Although the sandy soil of dune links is free draining there are places where the groundwater level is so high that damp or wet parts exist. These are called dune slacks and they attract their own selection of marsh-loving plants. Two plants are worth a special mention.

The **Flag Iris** (*Iris pseudacorus*) is present in this habitat in the east of our area, but very prominent in the west, where the high rainfall and high humidity allow it to prosper so that it becomes a

A Flag Iris flower. The plant occurs in many habitats, especially in the west

dominant and noticeable member of the plant community. It is also a component of the vegetation of riverbanks and marshes.

In the north and west of our area the **Baltic Rush** (*Juncus balticus*), though rather an unimposing green stalk, is important in showing that these dune links are strongly aligned botanically to the vegetation of the Nordic and Baltic plant communities. It can be found in very large colonies on Greenland Links in Caithness and in smaller groups scattered along the coast of the north and west. It is noticeable that the plants grow in straight

Baltic Rush – the delicate stems grow in a line

Cowslips

lines from a linear underground rhizome, while all other rushes grow in tufts. That makes it easier to know that you are looking at the correct rush.

On the north coast (and at Keiss Links, round the corner) there are **Cowslips** (*Primula veris*). This is somewhat remarkable because Cowslips are plentiful in England, becoming scarcer in the south of Scotland and absent from much of Scotland only to reappear on the north coast and Orkney Isles. Like the Primrose, the Cowslip has a basal rosette of leaves, but whereas the Primrose throws up many flowering stems from the base, the Cowslip puts up one sturdy stem which bears many flowers. In England the Cowslip has a preference for downland, but is common on many types of grassland and roadside verges; on the north coast it is specific to dune-links turf. The centre of its distribution is Strathy East, especially in the turf around the cemetery and on the steep cliff slopes where it was once very dense, though in recent years it has been reduced by heavy sheep grazing. The hybrid between the Primrose and the Cowslip is not uncommon where they grow together. It is intermediate in flower shape, often with a single flower stem that branches to show many flower heads.

ARCTIC-ALPINE COAST

North of Sandwood Bay the cliffs rise to form a plateau around 200 m high all the way to Cape Wrath and then along the north coast to Durness and Farr Bay. This stretch of coast has the characteristics of an arctic-alpine coast. Even down to sea level the flora contains species that are normally found on mountain tops or in the Arctic regions. These plants are the descendants of the plants that came in after the retreat of the ice at the end of the last ice age some 10,000 years ago.

The arctic-alpine landscape of the north-west with Mountain Avens

Moss Campion grows in tight hummocks on clifftops

In other places these plants were replaced by more vigorous and aggressive lowland plants as the climate warmed up, but here they remain in a climate harsh enough to deter the competitors.

On the bare clifftops the wind is strong enough to tear turf and peat from the rocky surface and the frequent rain washes nutrients from the soil. The Moine rock is also poor in nutrients so there is little yield of fresh minerals as the rock erodes. The characteristic plant that marks this as an arctic-alpine zone is

Moss Campion (*Silene acaulis*), typically growing in a tight cushion at the very edge of the cliff. Its pink flowers in July hardly protrude from the cushion on leafless stems. The easiest place to see this is on the cliffs at Cape Wrath or on the cliff just north of Sandwood Bay; there is a small amount on Fharaid Head by Durness.

At Durness the Moine rock is replaced by limestone. This is a more soluble rock and it releases a rich yield of minerals as it erodes so the soil is fertile and the rock is

weathered. Here the ground is overlain with sand from the beaches and it has become a dune links. Mostly it has been over-grazed in past times and lacks the species diversity that might be expected. However the golf course provides a spectacular display and there is a boggy area at the back of the village that has good plants around NC402669. South of the village there are some classic 'limestone pavement' formations though they are not particularly rich in plant species.

A few miles further east is the quite unique area of Invernaver and Bettyhill. Here the conditions have been ideal for the preservation of the relict arctic-alpine flora. The rock is a mica-schist which is a basic rock that erodes down to a mineral-rich sand, so plants thrive on the rock face, in the sandy turf and in the bare sandy places. The map on page 48 shows the more interesting places to visit.

On the grassy steep slopes there is a large colony of **Mountain Avens** (*Dryas octopetala*) with toothed leathery leaves which are white-felted on the back. The flowers have eight white petals and a yellow centre. The seeds are attached to long golden hairs. It is a plant of calcium-rich alpine soils and a good indicator of this type of soil. The plant is plentiful inland where the Durness limestone is exposed.

On the bare tidal sands there are large areas of **Yellow Mountain Saxifrage** (*Saxifraga azoides*) which is also plentiful along the banks of the burn. Its bright yellow flowers on stems some 10 cm high, with bright-green stem leaves, are prominent and add colour to the landscape. It likes wet places and is generally distributed in the north-west of our area.

The bare tidal sand at Invernaver is also the home of the tiny **Curved Sedge** (*Carex maritima*) which has a curved stem around 3 cm long and a cone-shaped fruiting head. In spring it is upright with a green head, but it lies prone on the sand with its seed head a prominent black in August. It is a rare plant in Britain and is easiest seen in our area. This site at Invernaver is one of the largest, with many thousands of plants although they do not all flower every year. It can also be seen in quantity in Caithness on Reay golf course and in the estuary of the small River Wester.

Rather less plentiful at Invernaver, but generally spread throughout the north and west, is the **Purple Mountain Saxifrage** (*Saxifraga oppositifolia*) which likes some mineral richness in the bare rock in which it lives and it likes the rock to be wet throughout the year. It is thus to be found prospering in shady places where it is not in direct sun. The easiest place to see it (it flowers in April or early May) is at Coldbackie on the north coast where it grows on the roadside rocks.

Invernaver is also a place to see the **Purple Oxytropis** (*Oxytropis halleri*) with its clustered head of purple pea-type flowers and divided hairy leaves. It is a high mountain alpine, but occurs as a relict of the last ice age in several places along the north coast (and a few scattered coastal places elsewhere). The best site is at Strathy East where it grows in quantity on the grassy cliff slopes.

Across the River Naver is the Invernaver Nature Reserve

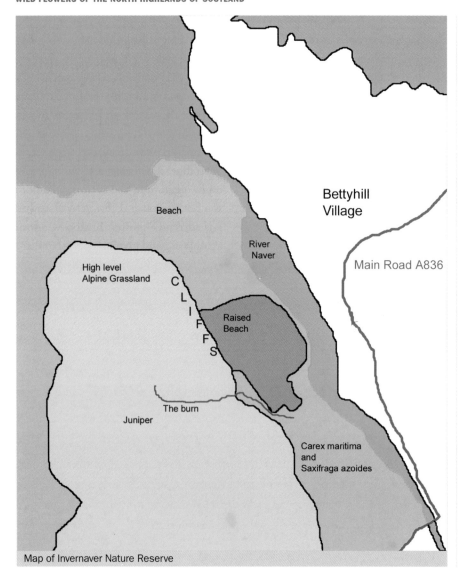

Map of Invernaver Nature Reserve

Another speciality of Invernaver is the **Dark Red Helleborine** (*Epipactis atrorubens*). It is a member of the orchid family and it grows in crevices in the steep cliffs and rather sparsely in the turf alongside the burn. It is about 20 cm tall with overlapping broad leaves on the lower stem, then a spike of dark-red

The Mountain Avens has leathery leaves felted with white on the back

Yellow Mountain Saxifrage

The Curved Sedge. Its flower head turns black when mature

hooded flowers above. It requires a rocky soil rich in calcium and minerals.

In the high-level dune-links turf at the north end of Invernaver is a rich display of the flowers mentioned previously as characteristic of dune-links turf.

The coastal arctic-alpine plants occur at scattered locations east of Invernaver, extending to Dunnet Head. **Alpine Saw-wort** (*Saussurea alpina*) grows at sea level on the cliffs one mile east of Thurso at ND141700. Its oval leaves, with undersides felted cotton-white, are evident throughout the growing season; the purple thistle-like flowers are on show during August. The duration of an individual flower is quite short; each head contains a mix of those coming out and those dying back so a fully 'out' head does not occur. Although it is something of a rarity as a coastal plant (it is also recorded at Invernaver), it is reasonably common as a component of our mountain flora and can be found on many of the hills in our area.

In addition to the larger, showier plants that inhabit this north-west corner of our area, it is rewarding to peer closely into the turf or the heath and see the plants that are living in the humid lower layer which provides some physical protection and shelter. For here there are rare mosses, liverworts and lichens,

Purple Mountain Saxifrage

Purple Oxytropis

Dark Red Helleborine at Invernaver

Alpine Saw-wort on the coast near Thurso

protrudes into the oceanic climate of the north Atlantic and provides a habitat unique in Europe; these more primitive plants, spread by spores instead of seeds, have filled the ecological niches rather faster than have the higher plants.

usually only 1 cm or less in size. This is the best habitat in Europe for this sub-layer of vegetation and the north-west mainland and the Western Isles are well recognised for this. Whereas the higher (vascular) plants are not as rich and diverse in Britain as they are in the rest of Europe, the mosses, liverworts and lichens are generally richer in our area. This is because the north of Scotland

Chapter 3. The Peatlands and other wet places

PEATLANDS

Caithness and Sutherland in particular are noted for their peatlands. Large areas of the land are covered in a layer of peat, most of which has accumulated during the past 5,000 years. It forms a very distinctive landscape and its surface is covered with specially adapted plants. Peat is not an hospitable environment for vegetation: it is usually waterlogged and devoid of oxygen; it is too soft and yielding to make a good rooting medium for forest trees and it lacks the essential foodstuff required by most plants. The plants specially adapted to prosper in these conditions are the main subject of this chapter. Other types of marshland, lochs and riversides are also covered.

To visit the peatlands is to experience space and quiet solitude. Because the land has no value for agriculture it has been left largely uninhabited. Here, it is often possible to be in a place where no other human is in sight, and where the calls of the red-throated diver and the golden plover set a plaintive background sound. Red deer move cautiously across the landscape in small groups and a short-eared owl quarters the ground, searching for small mammals. In this setting the plants are a further unique experience!

Sphagnum mosses are the most noticeable colonisers of wet peat and in their turn they are an important group of peat formers. When the mosses die they sink into the wet substrate and are replaced by a new generation of mosses.

But the old moss does not decay into humus in the way that dead grass or leaves recycle in normal soil. The wetness and lack of oxygen keeps the dead moss undecayed as a waterlogged fibrous mass and it simply accumulates as an ever-thickening layer which we call peat. Sedges and rushes are also a common component of the vegetation and they too die and form a layer of peat.

Peat formation is a one-way process. The material only remains as peat if the ground stays so wet that air is excluded. If the peat becomes drier then the process of decay will occur and the peat will be lost, either as plant food, as dust to be blown away or as soluble chemicals which can move with surface water. What is more, the peat is difficult to re-wet once it

Dubh Loch pools at Kensary in Caithness

Peaty pool pattern at Laxford Bridge; this is in a highly oceanic area

has become dry, reinforcing the drying out. So peat only accumulates reliably in places that are permanently wet, either because the weather is cool, cloudy, humid and rainy or because the groundwater is trapped in a basin of rock and is constantly kept at a sufficiently high level. Most of the good peatlands have both of these features.

The cool, cloudy, rainy weather comes from the proximity of the Atlantic Ocean and the frequency with which the air flows from the sea to the land. This is discussed in Chapter 7 and summed up in the word 'oceanicity'. In the present climate there is general peat formation over most of the countryside in the west of Sutherland where the oceanicity is high, but in the east of Caithness and east Sutherland the oceanicity is insufficient to maintain peat growth on drained surfaces though it still grows well in areas with a groundwater basin. This east–west difference in peatland vegetation is quite marked. While in the west there is abundant live peat formation, in the east there are large areas that formed peat in earlier times when the weather was wetter and now have a peat deposit which is permanently damp but not wet; here the peat is slowly decaying and carries a different flora.

In early times, a rock basin would have filled with water to become a loch. In the highly oceanic climate the edges of the loch would form peat and this would spread inwards to fill in the loch and form a peat basin. The continued formation of peat beyond this point is possible because the plants on the surface (especially the sphagnum mosses) draw water up to a higher level, acting like sponges. Also the layer of living plants and the roots of recently dead ones make the surface layer tougher and able to contain extra water in the basin, just as the skin of a rice pudding adds some stability to the whole. This raised bog is a delicate structure and easily damaged.

A good bog will have interesting pool patterns on its surface. For reasons which are not well understood the surface develops areas of bog pool. The dark, peaty, dubh lochs can be shallow or very deep with sharp margins between peat and water. The pools form complex patterns. The surface also develops hummocks formed by areas of sphagnum moss which grow upwards and draw up water; they can grow up to 1 m high containing a mixture of mosses, each adapted to exploit the conditions at a particular height in the hummock.

The activities of man have damaged many of these raised bog structures and caused them to leak and dry out. In the 1960s there was a campaign to drain bogs by cutting deep drainage ditches to expand the area of usable ground for agriculture. In the 1970s areas were deep-ploughed and planted with conifer trees. After that there was some recognition of the uniqueness and ecological value of the peatlands. Some repairs are currently being made by cutting down trees and blocking drains where they are causing severe leakage from a raised bog or excessive drainage.

There are still many good bogs to visit. At Forsinard the Royal Society for Protection of Birds has a large nature reserve with visitor facilities and guided tours. It is a good place to start, since one can see good peatland, be introduced to its plants and, importantly, do so in safety. For it must be recognised that bogs are dangerous places for the novice and there is a risk of becoming stuck in soft wet peat. We advise that visitors should not go alone and should take a stout walking stick to explore the ground ahead.

To see good views over the peatlands, two places are particularly worthwhile:

- Loch Lucy viewpoint, on the road between Helmsdale and Melvich at NC881397 gives a good view, from the lay-by at the roadside, across the peatlands of Achentoul with small lochs and pool systems and, in the background, the two hills Ben Griam Beg and Ben Griam Mor

- Ben Dorrery, ND062550, gives huge views to the west and south of the main part of the Caithness peatlands. It is a short climb along a good track from Dorrery Lodge at ND075550

To visit saturated peat with pools, go to:
- The RSPB reserve at Forsinard, where there are organised trails through wet peatland and the visitor does not cause lasting damage to the soft ground

- The Moine, to the south of Moine House at NC518600 which is on the road from Tongue to Durness. Here there is a good peatland close by the roadside

To walk on drier peat, visit:
- Yarrows Archaeological Trail starting at ND305432
- Dunnet Head, ND204765, which gives access to a range of wet and dry habitats as well as coastal turf, loch margins and some arctic-alpine species

PLANTS OF THE WET PEATLAND

Sphagnum mosses are a frequent component of bog vegetation. There are 25 species of sphagnum in our bogs and the differentiation of these is beyond our scope. They are all good at holding and retaining water – if a mass of the moss from above the groundwater level is squeezed it will reveal its large water content. The various species are adapted to differing conditions of water acidity, climate, oceanicity, exposure to sun and wind, etc., such that there is a species that will occupy each environmental niche in

Cottongrass in a peaty pool near Forsinard in Sutherland

Typical sphagnum moss on very wet peat; the green is *Sphagnum papillosum* and the red is *Sphagnum capillifolium*

Woolly Fringe-moss forms a hairy carpet

the peatland. When they die they form new peat; a large proportion of peat can be made up of these mosses. Because of its ability to soak up liquids, and having been taken from a sterile environment, sphagnum was collected and used as a wound dressing during World War One.

Woolly Fringe-moss (*Racomitrium lanuginosum*) is a moss with a grey woolly appearance. It is common on the tops of peat hummocks. It is also common on rocks in the uplands and mountains.

Round-leaved Sundew; it is often seen on bare peat as well as here in sphagnum moss

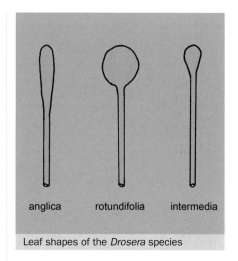

anglica   rotundifolia   intermedia

Leaf shapes of the *Drosera* species

Round-leaved Sundew (*Drosera rotundifolia*) is one of a family of insect-eating plants (the Sundews). They have green-and-red leaves with long red hairs. Each hair has a gland at its end which exudes a sticky liquid that glistens in the sunshine like a dewdrop (hence the name Sundew). If an insect should come in contact with the plant it gets caught in the sticky dewdrops which kill it and digest the soft parts of its body. The nutritious soup is absorbed into the plant and the insect husk blows away in the wind. This is a mechanism to allow uptake of nitrogenous food and some minerals that are absent from the peat. The Round-leaved Sundew can be distinguished by its leaf shape. It is very common on wet peat, especially where the water is static.

The **Great Sundew** (*Drosera anglica*) is distinguishable by its long Indian-club-shaped leaves which are at least four times as long as they are wide. Like the other species it has a white flower on a red stalk which rises well above the leaves. In this case the flower stalk arises from the centre of the basal rosette of leaves. The plant is common on wet peat and where there is flowing water at the edge of a raised bog or at the point where a small burn trickles into a loch. It is less common than the Round-leaved, but not as scarce as the **Oblong-leaved Sundew** (*Drosera intermedia*). It has a distinctive leaf shape,

Great Sundew growing in sphagnum moss

Leaves and flower of Atlantic Butterwort are pale colours

as shown here, but that is not sufficient to identify it. It also has a flower stem rising laterally from the side of the basal leaf rosette. It lives in wet bare peat in the higher rainfall areas of the west and is rare in the east.

In the west the **Atlantic Butterwort** (*Pinguicula lusitanica*) is another insect-eating plant of the wet peat. It has a rosette of basal leaves with a flower stem rising from the middle. At the top is a pale purple flower with a large lower lip. The leaves have sensitive hairs on the upper surface which, when stimulated by an insect, cause the leaf to roll up and enclose the insect. The leaf surface exudes digestive juices, digests the insect and opens to allow the husk to be blown away. This plant has a distinct preference for highly oceanic places, occurring west of

Bog Cranberry at Forsinard; this is *Vaccinium microcarpum*

Melvich and mainly on level saturated ground or west-facing slopes.

The **Bog Cranberry** (*Vaccinium microcarpum*) is a plant which is most often found on the margins of dubh lochs and wet hollows in the wettest peat. The stems trail across the peat, typically over an area of many square metres. These stems have pairs of opposite oval or round leaves; flowering stems rise at intervals along the creeping stems, bearing single magenta flowers with swept-back petals reminiscent of Cyclamen flowers. Red spherical cranberry fruits develop over the summer. There are two closely similar species – *Vaccinium oxycoccus* and *Vaccinium microcarpum* both of which have been reported in our area, though the latter is much more common.

The **Bog Asphodel** (*Narthecium ossifragum*) is another beautiful plant of wet peat. A member of the Iris family, it has sword-shaped leaves about 8 cm tall and a spike of elegant yellow flowers that bloom in August. Its Latin name ossifragum relates to the fact that the animals that graze on it frequently get brittle bones, probably because the whole habitat is deficient in calcium and a diet

Bog Asphodel

The Bog Orchid is rare and easily missed

based on plants from here leaves the animal without this vital mineral.

The rest of the plants of the wet peat are mainly sedges and rushes, which are better adapted to this environment than grasses. But you might find a Bog Orchid.

The **Bog Orchid** (*Hammarbya paludosa*) is small, typically 8 cm in height, and pale green with green-white flowers in a spike. There are small leaves at the base of the plant. It is scarce and mainly found in the west where it grows amongst sphagnum mosses, usually in a place where there is slight movement of the water. It is inconspicuous – there may be more of them than we think, waiting to be discovered!

PLANTS OF THE DRIER PEAT

The natural vegetation of drier peat is dominated by dwarf shrubs. Most common is **Heather** (*Calluna vulgaris*) with small purple flowers and small leaves in groups of four which overlap each other like slates on a roof. The flowers bloom in mid August to turn whole hillsides purple. Young seedlings are a few centimetres high and plants can live for

20 years or more, turning into small woody shrubs around 1 m high. This is the main food for grouse and deer, which nibble the young shoots. Known locally as 'muirburn', there is a tradition of burning old heather on the moor to release a supply of young shoots for the animals. Heather has been enormously important to the economy of the North Highlands. For more than 100 years, shooting estates have worked to achieve a monoculture of heather for grouse and deer sport, burning in controlled strips to achieve a mix of feeding and shelter for grouse. Crofters used heather for thatching, as a material for coarse ropes, as a mattress, and as food for bees producing heather honey. The uses to which heather has been put are many, ingeniously used by a people who had to employ what was abundantly available. White-flowered heather is thought to be very lucky!

There are two other Heaths – the **Bell Heather** (*Erica cinerea*) has deep pink, bell-shaped flowers and leaves in small bundles on the stem. It prefers a drier location than *Calluna vulgaris* and will normally occupy a dry knoll on the peat. The **Cross-leaved Heath** (*Erica tetralix*) has bell-shaped, pale pink flowers and

The 'Bonnie Purple Heather' of Scotland

Bell Heather likes a drier place

Cross-leaved Heath likes a wetter place

distinctive leaves in a cross of four at intervals along the stem. It likes a wetter place than *Calluna vulgaris* and is a common member of the wet-peat community.

There are three other common dwarf shrubs. The **Blaeberry** (*Vaccinium myrtillus*) has green ridged stems carrying ovate leaves with pinkish bell-flowers. On the open moor it chooses the best-drained places – especially steep slopes where water does not linger. But it is also the dominant plant in woods of Scots Pine where it carpets the peaty ground and it is very common in oak-birch woods on acid peaty soil. Its blueberry fruits taste wonderful. The **Cowberry** (*Vaccinium vitis-idaea*) has very similar flowers and bushy shape, but its leaves are rounded at the tip, where there is often a notch, and are more leathery to feel. It has bright-red berries. It is most at home in the medium-wet peat amongst the heather. Then there is the **Bearberry** (*Arctostaphylos uva-ursi*) which likes very dry, acid places and often creeps over dry rocks on the moors. With flowers and leaves similar to Cowberry it has to be distinguished by its more prostrate habit, or by observing that Bearberry has

Blaeberry flowers; note the grooved stem

Cowberry flower and fruit

Bearberry flowers

Crowberry

obvious veins on the underside of the leaf which are obscure in Cowberry.

The **Crowberry** (*Empetrum nigrum*) is not so shrubby. Its thin flexible stems creep amongst the heather and bear narrow shiny leaves around the stem. It has separate male and female plants and the females produce round berries which turn from green to black during the summer. The flowers are tiny and occur at the bases of the leaves.

The aforementioned four species have berries that are edible. There is a strong tradition of collecting Blaeberries for food, but not the other three. In contrast the Scandinavians, the Alaskans and the north Canadians take all these for winter food.

The **Lesser Twayblade** (*Neottia cordata*) used to be called *Listera cordata*. It is a tiny orchid which, in the common habitat of our area, is typically 5 cm high. It grows mostly under old heather shrubs. When the heather is 60 cm high it is often found by lifting up the heather and peering at the ground beneath. It is surprising how often this is successful.

The **Bog Myrtle** (*Myrica gale*) is a wonderfully fragrant dwarf shrub which will grow in wet or damp peat and

Lesser Twayblade flowers; it has two leaves at the base

The flowers of Bog Myrtle, which come before the leaves

Common Cottongrass

develops large colonies in places that it finds favourable. Its flowers and fruit are small and it has insignificant catkins (Bog Myrtle is botanically similar to Birch and Alder trees) so it is a matter of recognising the leaves which are grey-green and richly aromatic. It has been traditionally used to flavour beers (to replace hops) and was first choice as a 'natural' midge repellant. It was strewn

on floors so that the aroma arose when it was crushed and it was said to repel insects and keep the house clean. There is a continuing interest in the commercial possibilities of this plant.

There are some important sedges that deserve individual recognition. **Common Cottongrass** (*Eriophorum angustifolium*) is really a sedge, not a grass. It has fairly insignificant flowers in May arising from a far-creeping underground rhizome, so the flowering stems are spread around. In July the flowers produce seeds with long hairs which are the basis of the 'cotton' heads. This plant has more than one head of cotton on each plant. Another species is the **Hare's-tail Cottongrass** (*Eriophorum vaginatum*) which has only one cotton head per plant and the plants grow in tight clumps which often flop

The flower of Hare's-tail Cottongrass; a single head of silky hairs will come later

Deergrass in early summer with the anthers of the flowers prominent

down into a circle. Sheep readily eat Hare's-tail but not the Common Cottongrass.

Deergrass (*Trichophorum caespitosum*) is a single, thin green stem with a very insignificant flower and a tiny green leaf towards the base of the stem. It is worthy of mention because it is reasonably digestible to grazing animals and because there is so much of it on the peat. In the first frosts of autumn it turns a strong red which colours the moor on a large scale – especially the parts that were a bit too wet for heather domination and did not go purple earlier. Deergrass has a wide tolerance of wetness and appears in most parts of the moorland or peat bog.

Heath Rush (*Juncus squarrosus*) is one of the many inedible plants which are common in drier peat. Its stiff linear leaves form a prominent round tuft from which arises a central flower stem bearing unexceptional brown flowers.

Heath Bedstraw (*Galium saxatile*) grows to between 3 cm and 10 cm high

Heath Bedstraw

Heath Rush forms a tussock of inedible leaves

with tiny four-petalled flowers of pure white. The leaves are narrow and arranged in whorls of six (or so) around the stem. It likes the drier, better-drained hummocks and is also to be found around rocks.

Mountain Everlasting (*Antennaria dioica*) likes really well-drained conditions; on peatland it is usually found on a hummock or the margin by a rock. Otherwise it occurs on sandy ground such as exposed machair. There are separate male and female plants and the colour varies from white to pink.

Lousewort (*Pedicularis sylvatica*) has purple flowers in a tight leafy spike. The purplish leaves consist of many leaflets which are toothed and contorted. Its close relative, the **Marsh Lousewort** (*Pedicularis palustris*) likes much wetter conditions; it is a bit taller and is hairy just beneath the flower. The name 'lousewort' derives from an old belief that grazing animals got lice from eating the plant.

Mountain Everlasting

Lousewort

Common Milkwort (on Frizzled Crisp-moss)

Tormentil

Common Milkwort (*Polygala vulgaris*) and **Heath Milkwort** (*Polygala serpyllifolia*) look very similar and are both quite common. Heath Milkwort has at least some leaves in opposite pairs, whereas Common Milkwort has them all alternate. It is usual to have to get down low and peer at the lowest leaves to distinguish the two. Both have flowers of complex design which can be mauve, blue, pink or white. Milkwort is so called because it was believed that it increased the milk from a cow when eaten.

Tormentil (*Potentilla erecta*) is a very recognisable four-petalled (sometimes five-petalled, as in our illustration) yellow flower with leaves that are divided to look like a five-fingered hand. Its stems and leaves are finer than those of the Meadow Buttercup and it grows in great quantity on the drier moors. In the past its roots were used as a source of tannin for nets and leather.

Devil's-bit Scabious (*Succisa pratensis*) has a composite head of blue florets which appear in late summer.

Devil's-bit Scabious

Leaves and flowers of a female Creeping Willow

The plant likes damp or wet peaty places. It has a constriction at the base of the stem caused by the 'Devil's bite'.

Creeping Willow (*Salix repens*) would be very common on the dry peat, but it is grazed enthusiastically by deer and sheep and so kept in restraint. The leaves have silky hairs held tightly to the underside which make it easily recognisable amongst the willows. It is low-growing, usually 10 cm high. In spring the flowers appear in catkins, the male and female flowers being on different plants. The female flowers produce seeds in May which are dispersed on the wind, carried by long hairs. Masses of seed 'cotton' can sometimes be seen waiting for a fair wind to blow. There is a variety with silky hairs on both sides of the leaves that give the whole plant a distinctive silvery appearance; this variety is usually found near the sea on clifftop peat.

Eared Willow with typical ears and twisted leaf tips

Eared Willow (*Salix aurita*) is a shrubby plant usually around 1 m high which is frequent on the peat moor. The wrinkly twisted leaves are recognisable and they have two prominent 'ears' at the base of the leaf. Willows hybridise readily with any others nearby so it can be difficult to recognise some shrubs.

CALCIUM-RICH WETLANDS

Not all the waterlogged places are peaty and acid. Much depends upon the type of rock that underlies the soil or the type of rock in the vicinity whose groundwater drains to the wet place. If there is calcium in the rock or soil then the water will dissolve some of it and carry it to the wetland. Ten thousand years ago, after the glaciers melted, the soil would have been a mineral soil derived from the weathered rock. Over a long period of time, if well drained, it formed grassland and woodland; if not well drained then peat was formed, but in this case fen peat with calcium and other minerals present.

The main feature of fens is that there is plenty of plant food. The plants that grow here are tall herbs in dense clumps; such plants are tolerant of water-logging and are able to compete aggressively for space to grow. The places in our area with suitable rocks for fen development are on the Durness limestone of the Moine Thrust region in the west, and on the Old Red sandstone in the east. Limestone tends to dissolve away and form swamp holes which drain the fen, so it can only persist in small areas, whereas the Old Red sandstone has large areas of horizontal slabs which are virtually impermeable and very suitable for larger and longer-lasting fen formations – some important habitats of this type occur in Caithness.

The best examples of this type of habitat are (all in Caithness) the north-west side of Loch Watten, Loch of Durran, all the margins of St John's Loch, the north-west margin of Loch of Mey and the area round the Loch of Winless. In Sutherland parts of the Mound Alderwoods area are of this type. They are all treacherous places due to wet soft ground; the compact growth of the tall herbs makes walking difficult and shrubs grow amongst those to make the land yet more impenetrable. So please go carefully.

This type of vegetation merges into the wetter areas of the coastal machair and some plants are common to both. It also

Calcareous marsh with Flag Iris and Meadowsweet dominant

merges into wet woodland, river valleys and grassland to some degree and so species are shared with these habitats too.

Meadowsweet (*Filipendula ulmaria*) is a common tall herb in such a community. It has creamy-white flowers in foamy clusters. Close examination reveals white petals and numerous stamens but the overall effect is of a cloud of flowers. The leaves are divided into large and small sub-leaves which are opposite each other apart from the terminal one. Meadowsweet forms dense stands in wet places such as ditches, pond margins and mires where there is some calcium in the peat or soil. It has been used as a constituent of beer in former times and has various uses in herbal medicine.

Meadowsweet flower

Soft Rush in a damp meadow

The flowering head of Reed Canary-grass

Soft Rush (*Juncus effusus*) is the common tall rush of wet places. It has a single, tough green stem with a pointed end and a dark-brown flower cluster emerging from the side of the stem. The stems grow in a tight tuft. It is also at home in damp fields and grasslands.

Reed Canary-grass (*Phalaris arundinacea*) can be the dominant tall grass in this habitat. Reaching up to 2 m high, it has a tight flower spike and moderately broad leaves. Gardeners will perhaps know the variegated variety, Gardeners' Garters.

Common Reed (*Phragmites australis*) is even taller, reaching up to 3.5 m with a large spreading head of black flowers at the top. It is very aggressive and will dominate large areas of suitable ground. It can also be seen in the shallow water

Common Reed in a loch in west Sutherland

of a loch. Common Reed was always the preferred material for thatching houses; when the dead stems are cut in winter they make a thatch which is light, effective and lasting. Their harvest is not particularly damaging to the reed bed.

Two interesting grasses live in these tall herbs. **Narrow Small-reed** (*Calamagrostis stricta*) is a nationally rare grass, about 1 m high with a compact spike-like flowering head. It grows in quantity around the shores of St John's Loch in Caithness and in two other places in the county. The **Scottish Small-reed** (*Calamagrostis scotica*) also grows here. This one site is the only place in the world that it is known to occur, making it one of the rarest plants on the planet. It is only different from the Narrow Small-reed in certain details and there may be an argument for merging the two into just one species. But, for the time being, it is amongst the most special of plants.

Some attractive smaller plants are also found in the fens and mires, either in places where the tall herbs are not dominant or scattered amongst the tall herbs.

Narrow Small-reed at Watten, Caithness

Marsh Marigold at the edge of a river

Water Mint

Marsh Marigold (*Caltha palustris*) is a bright-yellow flower reminiscent of a large Buttercup. Its leaves are distinctively heart-shaped, so the plant is easily recognisable throughout the year. It occurs in many places that have permanent wetness and some calcium, such as river, burn and pond margins, wet woodland, fens and mires.

Water Mint (*Mentha aquatica*) is the only native mint locally and it too is to be found in the margins of rivers, burns and ponds, wet woodland, fens and mires. The minty perfume is delightful when the leaves are crushed.

Ragged-Robin (*Lychnis flos-cuculi*) has a loose cluster of pink or pale purple flowers on a single stem. The petals have a tattered appearance, hence the name. The plant is frequently found in fens and mires but also occurs in wet or damp meadows and on clifftops.

Ragged-Robin

Marsh Cinquefoil

Marsh Saxifrage

more calcareous, since the plant tolerates a fairly wide range of acidity.

Where peat overlies Old Red sandstone or Durness limestone there can be big differences in acidity. The surface water is strongly acid and chemically in balance with the peat. The water in the rock is calcareous because it has dissolved some of the minerals in the rock. When the water emerges from the rock at a fault or eroded surface feature it forms a calcareous spring. Usually this occurs on

An acid loch in west Sutherland with White Water-lily

Marsh Cinquefoil (*Potentilla palustris*) has an attractive flower with purple petals above green-and-purple sepals. Its leaves are cut into five separate leaflets. If you are standing by the plant you are most likely several inches deep in water. The water can be slightly acid or

a slope; the enriched water runs down the slope, altering the surface vegetation. This is called a calcareous flush. It produces a very noticeable local change of vegetation on a peat moor.

One such flush in Caithness, at the Munsary nature reserve, has the rare **Marsh Saxifrage** (*Saxifraga hirculus*). This plant is endangered throughout Europe and Caithness is a substantial and important site for the continuation of this species.

RIVERS AND LOCHS

As with marshes, the key consideration is whether a loch or river is acidic or calcareous. Calcareous water is clear and 'clean' in appearance; acidic water is brown and often cloudy. In calcareous water many useful nutrients are dissolved to supply plants with necessary food. In acidic water many useful nutrients are missing and the brown colouration is mainly due to organic matter suspended in the water that has not been broken down due to the absence of the appropriate bacteria and oxygen.

The plants that live in the water and on the shores are more numerous and varied if the water is calcareous, whereas if the water is acid, species are more restricted and specialised.

The biggest group is the **Pondweeds** (*Potamogeton* species) which root into the mud and have stems and leaves that are suspended in the water. They are to be found in acid or calcareous habitats and in still or rapidly flowing water. The flowers are simple unshowy structures, usually green or brown, which protrude from the water surface. There are about sixteen species and hybrids in our area. Some are difficult to determine and further detail is beyond the scope of this book.

Amphibious Bistort (*Persicaria*

A Pondweed flower protruding from the water

Amphibious Bistort

amphibia) has oval leaves with black blotches and a compact spike of small pink flowers. It can be seen as a fully aquatic plant invading calcareous lochs or as a constituent of the marsh vegetation, even lingering on in surprisingly firm and dry ground that has been drained.

The **White Water-lily** (*Nymphaea alba*) roots in mud from which it puts up its almost circular floating leaves and large, beautiful, white floating flowers with prominent yellow stamens. It is the only common Water-lily, and is especially frequent in the lochs of the west, becoming scarce in the east. The **Least Water-lily** (*Nuphar pumila*), with small yellow flowers, is only found in a few lochs in the higher ground between Lairg

White Water-lily

These are the flowers of the Branched Burr-reed

Water Lobelia with a basal shuttlecock of leaves below the water

and Rogart in east Sutherland.

There are several species of **Burr-reed** (*Sparganium* species). They have Iris-like leaves and some species can be taken for a group of Flag Iris. However, they all have flowers which look like spherical green or yellow globes and the leaves may be pliable and floating or stiff and erect.

In acid lochs the **Water Lobelia** (*Lobelia dortmanna*) has a shuttlecock ring of basal leaves on the loch bed submerged in around 15 cm of water. A single flower stem emerges from the water to display one or a few lilac flowers. It lives mainly in the west.

In water with some dissolved minerals the **Bogbean** (*Menyanthes trifoliata*) might be present. It survives in even quite acid water and the plant is a common feature of bog pools in the peatlands where the groundwater from a spring in the pool ameliorates the low mineral content of the peat water. Bogbean has trefoil-shaped leathery leaves and the most attractive white flowers fringed with white hairs. Later, a pod of yellow 'beans' develops. The roots can be in the substrate or floating in a raft on the loch surface. Bogbean is one of the most important plants of the Highland herbal tradition,

Flowers and leaves of Bogbean

being claimed to help many ailments. An extract of the roots is the usual medicine.

There are several species of sedge that inhabit the edge of the river or the margins of the loch.

The soil on the margins of lochs and rivers is usually a habitat in its own right. It can be shallow and marshy or can form a cliff high enough to isolate the plants on it from the influences of the river. But more commonly it is a modest bank, flooded when the water is high and drying out when the water is low.

A marsh attached to the edge of a large loch will be a stable, wet environment that never dries out. It can be a good home for long-living plants that cannot tolerate dry conditions. Perhaps that is the reason for the **String Sedge** (*Carex chordorrhiza*) growing in the marsh at the east end of Loch Naver. It was discovered by the bridge at Altnaharra in 1897 by two botanical friends, Rev. E.S. Marshall and W.A. Schoolbred; they toured the north several times around the turn of the century and made many botanical discoveries. It remained a mystery why this plant, frequent in mires in Russia, should be so uniquely sited in Britain. In 1978 it was discovered in a second locality

String Sedge shoot and fruiting head

in the great marsh attached to the south end of Loch Insh, near Aviemore. Today the sedge is still present at Altnaharra and can be seen at NC565361.

In general the marshy margins of a loch will reflect the amount of calcium in the habitat and will range from highly acid wet peat to rich calcareous marsh.

Higher banks, on river or loch, form a flood plain. This is an area which is periodically flooded but does not retain a high water table. The agitated water during flooding may bring extra oxygen to sweeten the soil, so it is less acid than adjacent peatland and less dry than adjacent grassland. Plants include many sedges, rushes and grasses and specialist marginal plants.

Globeflower (*Trollius europaeus*) is one of the most wondrous plants to come across when walking along a riverbank in early summer. In May and June the globular flowers are an exquisite lemon yellow, raising themselves on long stems above the light-green fresh foliage of the awakening riverbank. They are members of the Buttercup family as evidenced in the palmate divided leaves. In the west the plant also occurs – flowering a bit later – on wet ledges in ravines.

Globeflower

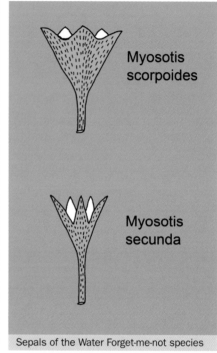

Myosotis scorpoides

Myosotis secunda

Sepals of the Water Forget-me-not species

Water Forget-me-not (*Myosotis scorpioides*) and **Creeping Forget-me-not** (*Myosotis secunda*) are very similar – both have blue flowers with yellow centres and white honey-guides on the petals. The flowers are about 8 mm diameter. The difference between the species is most obvious in the sepals behind the petals as shown in the diagram. With distinctly smaller flowers, only about

Water Forget-me-not

Sneezewort

One of the Monkeyflower hybrids

4 mm diameter, is the **Tufted Forget-me-not** (*Myosotis laxa*).

Sneezewort (*Achillea ptarmica*) is a composite flower, rather like a Daisy with its inner group of disc florets and an outer ring of 'petal' florets (the 'petals' are called ligules to be exact). It thrives in the damp turf of a riverbank or a calcareous marsh. The leaves cause sneezing when powdered.

Monkeyflower (*Mimulus* species and hybrids) originated in the Americas and, having been imported into Britain as a garden plant, has now invaded our rivers throughout the country. It is able to reproduce and spread by pieces of stem or root being carried by the stream to a new site. Most are hybrids with showy large flowers of yellow, red or copper, and the variation amongst populations in our area is considerable, though the hybrid *Mimulus guttatus* x *luteus* is the most common.

Water Avens (*Geum rivale*) is another marginal specialist. Its drooping flowers have pale pinky-purple notched petals wrapped with dark pinky-purple sepals. The leaves have pairs of lobes and usually a final lower pair of small lobes that make the plant easily recognisable. Where woodland meets waterside the Water Avens may interbreed with **Wood Avens** (*Geum urbanum*) whose flowers are yellow and not drooping. The result of the crossing is a plant halfway between;

Water Avens

Wood Avens

Common Valerian

Holy Grass

it is one of the most common hybrids and is called *Geum* x *intermedium*.

Common Valerian (*Valeriana officinalis*) has an umbel head of flowers which are a distinctive shade of bluish-pink. The leaves also are distinctive, having (usually) nine toothed leaflets. It is a frequent inhabitant of the riverbank or marsh.

On the banks of the Thurso River is the rare **Holy Grass** (*Hierochloe odorata*) which looks like an ordinary meadow grass but for its shining seed cases. It occurs in many locations on the riverbank south of Thurso town and was found there around 1830 by Robert Dick. He was a local baker, self-trained in botany and geology and the discoverer of much of the Caithness flora. He is celebrated by the Victorian sociologist Samuel Smiles who published in 1878 the book *Robert Dick, Geologist and Botanist* in his series of tracts on the virtues of self-help and the benefits of reading and study. Dick's discovery of the grass was the first authenticated find of the plant in Britain. It is common in Scandinavia but rare in Britain and may have been imported by Vikings since it is found today in sites which were colonised by the Norsemen. In Scandinavia it was strewn on the floors of churches for the benefit of worshippers because, when crushed, it emits the pleasingly sweet scent of newly-mown hay.

Chapter 4. Woodlands

INTRODUCTION

If nature were left alone to develop the vegetation of the North Highlands, then, eventually, many places would be covered with woodland. For a large part of Scotland the natural woodland would be dominated by oak and birch, some would be pinewood and then there would be special types of woodland to suit special places. In reality much of this natural woodland has not developed or has been removed. To a large extent this is because woodland is a type of vegetation where human activity has had a big impact. The impact has been evident over the last 5,000 years, so the story is complex and not easy to interpret. Today the North Highland area has mere fragments of natural woodland. They are often interesting and rewarding to visit and are sufficient to illustrate and portray the range of woodlands that would prosper without human intervention.

Woodland types are determined mostly by the type of soil and the summer temperatures and rainfall. Not only do these factors decide the species of trees that can prosper and dominate, but they also determine the ground flora that can prosper underneath the trees. It is usually easier for a botanist to recognise a type of woodland by looking at the ground flora than by looking at the trees alone, for the ground flora supplies many more clues. There is a subtle interaction to be considered. The established trees take up water and nutrients from the soil, tending to dry and impoverish it. They allow light to the forest floor during winter and then shade it to a varying degree during summer. They shed leaves which compost down to enrich the soil. The acidity of the soil derives from the natural acidity of composted leaves and the release of calcareous minerals from the soil or the groundwater. The ground flora is composed of those plants that prosper in the given shade, wetness, acidity and soil enrichment. These are all delicate balances which change markedly from place to place and make the interpretation of woodland a most fascinating exercise.

Human interference with woodland commonly takes one or more of the following forms:

Big Burn Wood at Golspie with Ransom's Garlic and Wild Hyacinth

Birch and Aspen beside a burn

Young and mature female cones on a Larch branch

- Clear felling and replanting, often with an 'improved' variety or a quite different species. This leaves the old ground flora below new trees, at least for a while
- Changing the ground flora grazing regime, usually to over-graze the ground and prevent new seedlings from developing so the wood has only old trees and eventually none when they die out
- Planting blocks of alien trees (such as Larch or Lodgepole Pine) adjacent to a natural wood, so that the aliens merge in and perhaps take over
- Harvesting the wood by coppicing, which keeps the trees alive but in an immature form and alters the amount of shade that they cast
- Clearing the ground totally for a new use such as agriculture or housing
- Ploughing and planting, which creates a new drainage regime and a different type of habitat for as long as the drainage is functional

The woodlands of our area have been immensely important historically to the economy and culture of its people. When the woods were dense they inhibited travel, got in the way of agriculture, sheltered wolves, provided a ready source of building material and provided a diversity of food. Mainly in the seventeenth century the woods were cleared by commercial and naval interests and in the ensuing years open space for agriculture was preferred to woodland. The coming of the sheep farms around 1810 produced a regime in which seedlings were grazed and forest regrowth was suppressed.

THE OAK-BIRCH WOODS
On Neutral Soil

The natural wood of deep-brown forest soil with some shelter from high winds and moderate rainfall has, as principal components, the Sessile Oak and the Downy Birch with Wood-sorrel in the ground flora. There are distinct variations in our area. There is more oak in the mixture in the south and west with no oak at all, just birch, north of Brora in the east, and north of Kylesku in the west. The lack of oak in the northerly version of the wood is predominantly because acorns rarely mature here during the cool summers. This may have been helped

West-coast woodland at Unapool, Sutherland

along by the few existing oaks being cut down, so reducing further the seed bank in the soil. Now there are no seeds to allow regeneration even during a warm summer. There is also an east–west gradient of the oak species. In the east it is predominantly Sessile Oak, while in the west it becomes predominantly Pedunculate Oak with hybrids of the two species very common. There is also a similar east–west gradient of birch, with Downy Birch exclusively in the west and a mixture with Silver Birch in the east (with, again, hybrids between the two being common).

Sessile Oak (*Quercus petraea*) is a long-lived tree with a straight trunk.

A hybrid close to Pedunculate Oak; the pure species would have longer acorn stalks and shorter leaf stalks

A hybrid close to Sessile Oak; the pure species would have longer leaf stalks

Its lobed leaves have a long leaf-stalk, usually about 12 to 25 mm in length. The acorns have a short stalk of up to 20 mm long. It tolerates acid soil and wetness very well but does not venture north as far as the Pedunculate Oak, probably because it needs more warmth to ripen its acorns.

Pedunculate Oak (*Quercus robur*) is a long-lived tree with a less straight trunk than the Sessile Oak and with main branches more spreading. Its lobed leaves have a short leaf-stalk, usually only about 2 mm long. The acorns have a long stalk, maybe 50 mm, so that the stalk and cupule look like a miniature clay pipe.

An old, gnarled Downy Birch with Bracken Fern below

A mature Silver Birch; note the drooping ends of the branches

Downy Birch (*Betula pubescens*) is a tree of moderate or short stature – generally getting shorter and stouter as one moves north. Its trunk is shiny brown when it is young, becoming grey or white later, but it doesn't have the strongly contrasting white-with-black fissures of the Silver Birch. The twigs at the ends of branches are upright or ascending. Leaves are oval and either simply toothed or not consistently doubly-toothed. This is the common and widespread tree of the North Highland area, tolerating peaty acid soil, wetness and shallowness.

Silver Birch (*Betula pendula*) is a tall tree with a straight trunk of silver-white bark erupting into black fissures and bosses below. The twigs at the ends of main branches hang down pendulously. Leaves are more pointed than the Downy Birch and have obvious double serration – teeth with teeth on them. In the pure form it is most common in the south-east around Golspie and Dornoch. It hybridises readily with Downy Birch and there can be large stands of trees that cannot be categorised as either species.

Hazel (*Corylus avellana*) is often an important component in this type of wood. It occurs where there is a bit more mineral richness in the ground and a botanist might look more carefully at the ground flora near Hazel since the richness

Leaves and immature nuts of Hazel

Leaves of Aspen with the long, thin leaf stems

often brings more diversity of ground flora species. Hazel is a shrub, having multiple main stems, and does not compete with the taller trees for a place in the wood canopy. In spring the male catkins are prominent, spreading pollen in the wind for the small female flowers. The fruit is an edible nut which was obviously a mainstay of the diets of early people. It does not regularly ripen in the far northern summer.

Aspen (*Populus tremula*) is a tree of variable stature depending on the situation. It does not produce seed in our current climate, so the plants reproduce and extend themselves by suckering. Underground creeping roots throw up new shoots which become the new trees. The climate has not been suitable for sexual reproduction for the last few thousand years so the existing trees are clones of those that invaded the habitat a long time ago. There are dwarf Aspen trees clinging to the very cliff-edge on the north coast (Dunnet Head is a good place to see these), there are well established colonies of woodland Aspen at Dunbeath and in the west-coast woods, and there are many more in scattered small groups across our area. This tree has round, toothed leaves on long, flattened leaf-stalks which flutter in the lightest breeze and give rise to an alternative name – Trembling Poplar. It is found in woods with rich mineral soil, but also in upland areas along rocky streams and chasms.

Gean or **Wild Cherry** (*Prunus avium*) is a medium-sized tree with a shiny reddish-brown trunk and oval, toothed leaves. It has prominent white flowers in May which make it stand out in the woodland setting. The fruit is a small red or black cherry hung in clusters from a single point on the stem. It needs to be differentiated from the **Bird Cherry** (*Prunus padus*) which is also a frequent medium-sized tree with a purplish peeling bark. The white flowers are in a prominent spike in May and they give rise to black cherry-like fruits which are attached at intervals along the stem of the spike. The photographs show the difference in flower arrangements. Both avoid the most acid soil and are comfortable when it is neutral. They occur throughout our area.

Typical plants in the ground flora are as follows.

Wood-sorrel (*Oxalis acetosella*) is immediately recognised by its trefoil leaf (which is a lighter green than clover and the leaflets fold down the middle). The flower is white and is to be found in May. It has a strong preference for a fertile, not-too-acid woodland soil and may persist if the trees die out. It is a good indicator of a former birch wood when found on open ground.

Wild Hyacinth or **Bluebell** (*Hyacinthoides non-scriptus*) is the plant

Gean

Bird Cherry

Wood-sorrel with its folded trefoil leaves

that carpets the woods of England and southern Scotland in the spring. In Scotland one is careful about the name since *Campanula rotundifolia* is preferably called the 'Bluebell'. Wild Hyacinth is in fact a scarce plant in the European context and Britain has most of it. In our area it is found in only a few woods (for example the Big Burn at Golspie) but nevertheless it occurs widely and there are some patches of complete spring domination and many places where it is found in small pockets and scattered on roadside verges. It likes a deep, moist soil.

Wood Anemone (*Anemone nemorosa*) is also a powerful carpeter of woodland floors further south, but it is commonly only found in the southern half of our area. It likes a drier wood than the Wild Hyacinth and will put up with a shallower soil. Although it has an early white flower like Wood-sorrel, the Wood Anemone has a lobed leaf quite unlike that of Wood-sorrel.

Common Dog-violet (*Viola riviniana*) is our most common violet. It has a heart-shaped leaf and a medium-sized purple flower. It is widespread in grassland and woodland in places where the soil is not very acid.

Lesser Celandine (*Ranunculus ficaria*) is a member of the Buttercup family. It throws up yellow flowers in early spring – February or March depending on the number of mild days – and the flowers can linger on into May. The leaves appear at the same time; they are shield-shaped and dark green with black blotches. There are two forms: a form which has bulbils which develop at the soil surface level and multiply rapidly to give a very invasive plant which can cover

Wild Hyacinth thrives in a wood with rich soil

Wood Anemone flower

Common Dog-violet

Lesser Celandine – the variety that spreads by bulbils

Wood Sage

woodland floors (and the soil of gardens!) and a form which does not grow bulbils and occurs in small scattered groups mainly on acid grassland.

Wood Sage (*Teucrium scorodonia*) has distinctive wrinkled leaves and pale greenish-yellow flowers. It prefers upland woods and rocky knolls and will live on a wide range of acid and alkali soils.

Greater Stitchwort (*Stellaria holostea*) has handsome white flowers, each with five bifid petals. Oak-birch woodland is its natural home, but it persists in grassland if the wood is cleared so is now common in roadside and hedgerow grass and along riverbanks. The east coast between Helmsdale and Berriedale has a particular concentration of this species in grassland which was formerly woodland.

Germander Speedwell (*Veronica chamaedrys*) is a sprawling plant with brilliant azure-blue flowers, each with a white eye. A good check to distinguish it from other species of Speedwell is that the white hairs on its stems grow in two lines on opposite sides. It too persists in cleared woodland and has become a common component of the roadside verge flora.

Primrose (*Primula vulgaris*), with its intense yellow flowers, puts on a show in late spring. It remains in the roadside verges and unimproved grassland as a relict of former woodland. It is also common on grassy sea cliffs and is quite tolerant of moderate salt deposition.

Foxglove (*Digitalis purpurea*) populates the margins and clearings of woodland as well as stony banks and disturbed ground. The pink-purple flowers are indeed like the finger-ends of gloves. The name derives from 'folks-glove' – the glove of the fairy-folk.

Greater Stitchwort – other species of
Stitchwort also occur

Germander Speedwell

Primrose

An extract of *Digitalis* made from the plant is an established medicine for heart complaints.

Honeysuckle (*Lonicera periclymenum*) is a woody climbing plant which twines clockwise through other shrubs and also clings to rocky outcrops and creeps along the ground in shady places. It prefers drier or well-drained sites. The flowers are two-lipped and light yellow inside when young, turning more orange when pollinated. The outside is crimson to a greater or lesser degree. It is common at wood margins and on steep rocky ground.

Ivy (*Hedera helix*) is also a woody climber, though it grips with rootlets on the stems rather than twining. It is found climbing up and swamping trees and it also covers ground. The comprehensive cover of its numerous dark-green leaves excludes the light and restricts any competitive growth from other plants. Its flowers are green, with yellow anthers and they appear in November, mature through the winter and produce a black berry. The progress that it makes with its winter flowering varies with the weather. The plant is very hardy and salt-tolerant and is not uncommon on sea cliffs and geos.

Foxglove

Honeysuckle

Moschatel (*Adoxa moschatellina*) is an unusual plant just 5 cm high, which has five tiny green flowers at right angles to each other like the faces of the town hall clock. It also has trefoil leaves, with one pair to each flower stalk. It grows in the richer woods in the south and east of our area – Rogart, Golspie Big Burn, Dunbeath Valley and particularly Latheronwheel Burn valley.

Shuttlecock-shaped fern plants are a feature of the woods. The individual species are not easy to distinguish. The most frequent one is the **Broad Buckler Fern** (*Dryopteris dilatata*) which has triangular dark-green fronds and the lower stem has scales with a very dark-brown stripe. It occurs in many habitats, not being confined to woods. The **Golden-scaled Male Fern** (*Dryopteris affinis*) has a frond shaped like an African shield, is a medium-green colour and the base of the stem is clothed in dense golden scales. It is common in woods but also common along roadside verges. In wetter places the **Lady Fern** (*Athyrium filix-femina*) also has a frond shaped like a shield and it has lots of less brightly coloured scales on its stem. Overall it is more finely divided than the Golden-scaled Male Fern and the individual leaflets of the frond have sharp teeth.

Ivy flowers in early winter

The tiny flower head of Moschatel

Broad Buckler Fern

A frond of Golden-scale Male Fern

Woods on Acid Soil

There is also a natural oak-birch combination which develops on peaty acid ground. It too is dominated by Sessile Oak and Downy Birch, but Wood-sorrel is absent (as well as others of the ground flora species listed above). This type of wood has a ground flora typified by Blaeberry, Heather and other acid-loving species. It is the more common type of wood in the north and west where the higher rainfall, higher humidity, harder rocks and thinner, more peaty, soils prevail. In the wettest places the trees are coated with mosses and lichens and the woodland floor also has a rich moss and liverwort element.

Rowan (*Sorbus aucuparia*) is an occasional companion to the dominant trees, particularly in the north-west. Its leaf is a compound leaf of about 13 leaflets. Its white flowers produce bright-red berries. It is a very adaptable shape, being able to grow tall when among tall trees and to grow multi-stemmed as a shrub in more scrubby situations. Its young seedlings are susceptible to grazing, which limits its success. Traditionally it was thought to afford protection against witches and that

A typical northern Rowan tree

Holly often grows by a fast-flowing burn in the west

a tree in the yard or a bough over the door or fireplace would protect people and farm animals from becoming bewitched.

Holly (*Ilex aquifolium*) is a shrub which is also susceptible to grazing, despite its leathery, prickly leaves. It succeeds best in the humid north-west on rocky outcrops and gorges.

Bracken (*Pteridium aquilinum*) is often present in this type of wood, though only where there is deep soil and sufficient moisture. It is a very persistent fern and attempts are often made to eradicate it

because both the juice when its ferns are damaged and the spores that are released in late summer when it is brushed by animals or people are highly carcinogenic. Notice that it has branched stems while the other common ferns have a single central stem.

Hard Fern (*Blechnum spicant*) is distinctive because its fern blades are singly divided and the spores appear only on some thinner, inner 'fertile' blades. Its blades arch out from a single growing point and often reach 1 m in height in a

sheltered shady wood. It also occurs commonly in peatlands where it grows in the open moor and is much more compact.

Great Wood-rush (*Luzula sylvatica*) grows in large tufts of tough leaves. The dull-brown rush flowers rise above them on tall, dark, tough stems. The leaves are the preferred lining material for a golden eagle's nest. The plant can grow in extensive mats in woodland and typically occupies ledges on steeper ground and rocky outcrops.

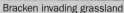
Bracken invading grassland

Hard Fern on peaty ground

Slender St John's Wort (*Hypericum pulchrum*) is noted for its elegance. The flower petals are yellow above, red beneath and edged with red and black dots. It usually grows in small groups on the drier, moderately acid ground in the type of wood we are considering, on open peat moor and on grassy banks. It is usually in flower on the date (24 June) taken to be the birthday of St John the Baptist. The plant is traditionally important in Highland medicine and is said to bring peace and happiness to those who wear a bunch under the left armpit. A closely related species, *Hypericum perforatum* is used in modern times as an antidepressant medication.

The best example of neutral-soil, oak-birch woodland which contains a good proportion of oak is just west of Spinningdale, where it is on either side of the road. An excellent contrast to that is the acid soil oak-birch wood at Loch a' Mhuilinn on the west coast. There are many patches of Downy Birch wood without any oak along Strath Ullie and Strath Halladale, growing on acid or neutral soils with well-developed ground flora. Richer soils with Hazel occur in Dunbeath Strath. The west coast has many examples of the Downy Birch wood in wet acid conditions at, for example, Drumbeg, Nedd, Inverkirkaig and Inverpolly. On the north coast there are good examples at Tongue, on the flanks of Ben Hope and at Armadale Burn.

Great Wood-rush flower head

Slender St John's Wort

Balblair Pinewood near Golspie

SCOTS PINE WOODLAND

Pine forests do best where summers are cool and moderately wet while winters are cold and snowy. In Scotland, therefore, pine's natural region is the area around the Cairngorm plateau and immediately south of the Moray Firth. Such a habitat is also present in the south-east of our area and is of sufficient interest and distinction to be worthy of inclusion. Here, the dominant tree is the Scots Pine and the dominant shrub is Juniper. The best example is at Balblair Wood just south of Golspie.

Scots Pine (*Pinus sylvestris*) is a tall tree with orange-brown bark above and grey flaking bark below. It has grey-green needles in pairs. The natural Scottish form has a sinuous trunk with heavy side branches, though these side branches are brittle and liable to fall off during storms or heavy snow. The top of the tree has a pyramidal shape. Foresters have bred a tree with a straight trunk, fewer smaller side branches and a flat top to the crown when it is mature. Since many native trees have been harvested and replaced with foresters' trees, the latter are now in the majority.

Juniper (*Juniperus communis*) is a shrub reaching 5 m in height with many spreading branches. Its needles are single,

A mature native Scots Pine tree

Juniper with first-year berries

pointed and have a white band on the upper side. The female flower is a cone that produces a round berry which is initially green for the first year, then turns purple-black as it matures on the shrub for the second or third year. It occurs mostly in pinewood, but is also a constituent of the oak-birch woodland and it is scattered throughout the north in such woods or as a relict of former woods. On the north and west coasts the Prostrate Juniper (*Juniperus communis* subsp. *nana*) is to be found staying low in the heather on exposed clifftops and upland heaths.

The ground flora of the Scots Pine wood is quite distinctive. Fallen pine needles decay very slowly, so the forest floor, on a sandy or gritty base, consists of a thick layer of partly decayed needles. It is a very acid medium so the primary ground flora consists of three acid-loving dwarf shrubs – Heather, Blaeberry and Cowberry. Among these dominant plants we can find the following species.

Twinflower (*Linnaea borealis*) is a low creeping undershrub with opposite pairs of leaves. The flowers rise on a single stalk, from which hang two perfect pink bells. This rare beauty was the favourite flower of Carl Linnaeus, the great Swedish botanist. It occurs in two substantial colonies in Balblair Wood at Golspie. It is nationally rare.

St Olaf's Candlestick (*Moneses uniflora*) is one of the wintergreens, and a

The exquisite Twinflower

One-flowered Wintergreen, or St Olaf's Candlestick

Creeping Lady's Tresses

rare species in Britain, though it is circumpolar in the conifer forests of the north. From a rosette of basal leaves arises a single stem shaped like a swan's neck, terminated by a single flower of pure white with yellow stamens, a green ovary and a prominent green style. It occurs in small colonies among the sparse heather and moss of the forest floor. It is in Balblair Wood in scattered groups.

Creeping Lady's Tresses (*Goodyera repens*) is a small white-flowered orchid with a creeping stem which spreads the plant through the top layer of fallen pine needles and decayed mosses. There are around 20 small white flowers in a loose spike at the top of a light green stem. It occurs in several wooded areas around Golspie, being plentiful in Balblair Wood.

VARIATIONS ON THE THEME

The oak-birch and pine woodlands are the prime types in our area. There are some important variations to be considered.

On Limestone

The presence of limestone in a band southwards from Durness presents the

The black bud at this Ash branch tip has produced flowers, then seeds and then leaves

opportunity for some woodland to be on the calcareous soil derived from the limestone. The natural development would be the upland ashwood which is dominated by Ash and Hazel and has a ground flora which includes Dog's Mercury. An important point about limestone soil is that it encourages a wider range of species to grow, so a diversity of tree and shrub species is to be expected. In fact the upland ashwood is not achieved in our area, the nearest proper

development being at Rassal at the head of Loch Kishorn in Wester Ross. The scraps of woodland that do occur on the limestone and calcium-rich sandstones are oak-birch woods that contain Rowan, Hazel, Ash and Wych Elm as extra species. In a few places natural dense Hazel scrub is formed.

Ash (*Fraxinus excelsior*) is a substantial tree with twigs easily recognised by the shape of the terminal bud. The leaf is compound, having about 11 leaflets.

111

Woodruff

Hartstongue Fern

The flowers come out before the leaves and yield seeds with a single membranous wing to carry them away in the breeze. Its preferred habitat is nutrient-rich soil and it is widely planted on good soil.

The ground flora on limestone and other rich soils is more diverse and might include these extra species.

Woodruff (*Galium odoratum*) has whorls of about six leaves around the stem, topped by a cluster of tiny white flowers. It prefers rock outcrops and well-drained banks in the wood; it is common on limestone in the west and on rich sandstone (such as Dunbeath Valley) in the east.

Hartstongue (*Phyllitis scolopendrium*) is a fern with a whole undivided blade. The spores are in oblique rows on the back of the blade. It is frequent in the west, scarce on the north coast and virtually absent from the east. Because of its liking for lime, it is also found on mortared walls in damp shady situations throughout the area.

In Wet Places

The oak-birch wood can extend into some particularly wet places. When this happens Alder and Willow become significant or major elements in the wood. The Alder tends to take over when the ground is level and permanently saturated. The Willow predominates when the ground is sloping and wet

Female Alder catkins in late summer

Grey Willow catkin in spring

Goat Willow catkin and leaf buds

Ramsons garlic

Golden Saxifrage in spring

(or the groundwater is flowing for some other reason) – for example where a stream passes through a rocky wooded gorge.

Alder (*Alnus glutinosa*) is a shrub or small tree that has a distinctive round leaf with a blunt or indented tip. It has long, drooping male catkins with lemon-yellow anthers and small spherical female catkins with red styles which turn into black spheroidal fir-cone-like fruits that persist all year. It prefers a permanently wet soil and is common on marshes, riverbanks and edges of lochs.

There are several species of Willow that occur in wet woods. One feature of Willows is that the buds have one outer scale, so are appressed to the twig. Also the trees are either male or female. The most common is the **Grey Willow** (*Salix cinerea* subsp. *oleifolia*), a medium-sized shrub with oval leaves inrolled at the edges which have distinct rust-coloured hairs on the back. The **Goat Willow** (*Salix caprea*) has almost round leaves and prominent male catkins in the spring.

The ground flora in the wet places is also distinctive.

Ramsons (*Allium ursinum*) is the common wild garlic. In woods with richer soil it is to be found in wet places such as the low bank of a burn, river or ditch. The large, strongly scented, spathe-like leaves are topped by a spherical cluster of white star-like flowers in May.

Golden Saxifrage (*Chrysosplenium oppositifolium*) covers the wettest soil with round-lobed leaves in opposite pairs and bright-yellow small flowers in April.

Melancholy Thistle (*Cirsium heterophyllum*) is distinctive because its thistle-like purple head is combined with leaves that are not spiny and have a white cottony underside. When young, the heads droop, gradually coming upright with age. This has given rise to the

Melancholy Thistle

'melancholy' tag. It occurs in groups alongside burns in the west and south-east.

ALIEN WOODS

There are various kinds of woodland that have been artificially created in our area for either commercial or decorative reasons.

Wood was removed without replacement until the mid nineteenth century, by which time there was a recognition that the supply of wood had to be 'sustainable'. It has since become the practice to plant new trees, the motives and incentives being variable over the years.

Policy woods often surround a large house which is part of an 'estate'. They were planted to last and the typical species are Beech, Sycamore, Oak, Ash, Scots Pine, Norway Spruce and Silver Fir. Many such policies are still in good condition.

Some natural woods were 'improved' or extended by adding alien trees. The species listed above for policy woods are typically those added. Sycamore and Swedish Whitebeam have proved to be remarkably resilient survivors in the most

Bud bursting on a Sycamore tree

exposed places. They spread by self-sowing in the warmest summers but often in normal years the seed does not mature in our northern parts.

Relatively small areas became planted as shelter belt. These usually appear in open country at the edge of a farm (for sheltering sheep and cattle), on heather moor (for sheltering deer) or along roads and railways (to prevent snowdrifts). To provide low-down shelter the trees have to have branches right down to the ground, so the pyramidal conifers such as Norway Spruce are preferred.

After 1945 and mainly in the 1970s it became the practice to plant large blocks of conifer trees. There were tax incentives to encourage the planting. The purpose was to gain useful exploitation of 'useless' ground, to create a new industry of commercial forestry for softwood timber and paper-making and to create the long-term prospect of employment in industries which use timber. Large forests of closely planted Lodgepole Pine and Sitka Spruce were established on open, coarse, acid grassland, heather moor and blanket peat bog. These forests are now coming to a mature state and some are being felled. The trees are so close that they shade out any ground flora and the fallen needles acidify the soil, so there is little of botanical interest.

Plantations of alien conifer trees in Sutherland

Chapter 5. Grasslands and Uplands

INTRODUCTION

When left to nature, good bare mineral soil will develop into grassland and then into woodland, so grassland is a condition in which the onward progress to woodland has not occurred. That is often due to human activities, especially grazing of animals on the ground. However, in our area there can also be climatic suppression of woodland due to high winds, salt spray or cool summer conditions inhibiting seed development. Grasslands divide into those heavily managed by farmers and those more natural ones associated with upland and mountain areas as well as, in our case, some coastal clifftops. We consider the former in Chapter 6 and here consider the latter – very large areas of ground that are too elevated or exposed for intensive farming. In the east these areas are associated with low hills and in the west they can be part of the dramatic and picturesque mountains for which the area is rightly famed.

Upland and mountain peaty terrain makes up an even larger extent of land. It is considered here since it is an extension of the peatland into the high mountains. And of course the mountain-top plateaux and the mountain cliffs are special types of habitat that have their own flora.

There are many wonderful mountains in our area, worthy of a lifetime's exploration. They are treasured for the superb landscape that they create, explored for the wealth of geological interest that they represent, and are a source of fascination for plant-hunters because this is the north-west corner of Europe, protruding into the oceanic climate of the Atlantic.

Particularly good areas to explore are the limestone exposures at the Inchnadamph cliffs, and the mountain slopes of Conival and Ben More Assynt. Other areas are not so rich, but Ben Klibreck, Quinag and the west cliff of Ben Hope offer good hunting. The smaller mountains to the east are also interesting, especially Ben Griam Beg and Morven. Outside the mountains proper the cliffs, gullies and ravines all over the area provide a little shelter and will often be rewarding.

The mountain Glas Bheinn viewed from Inchnadamph cliffs; the foreground is on Durness limestone rock

Inchnadamph cliffs are of Durness limestone

GRASSLANDS

Much of our natural grassland is in the uplands. This is the sort of grassland that develops naturally because climatic conditions are too harsh for trees to grow and the ground is too dry or well-drained to encourage peat formation. There is, of course, plenty of grassland at all altitudes because crofters, farmers and estate owners keep ground in a grassy state for grazing. It can be in any condition ranging from a monoculture of agricultural grasses to a rich, interesting mix of natural species.

The biggest influence on the nature and quality of grassland is the amount of calcium in the soil. It is usual to grade soils as peaty, neutral or calcareous. Of course grasslands also merge into other habitats. Wet peaty grassland easily becomes peat moorland. Wet calcareous grassland becomes fen. Sheltered grassland becomes oak-birch woodland. Sandy grassland becomes machair.

The scope of this book does not include detailed discussion of the grasses, sedges and rushes that are the major constituents of grassland, but there are other plants that belong in this habitat.

The **Dandelion** (*Taraxacum* species) is not just a single species, it is a complex of microspecies. Most British Dandelions reproduce by apomixis – that is they produce viable seed without the need of fertilisation and so their offspring are exact replicas of themselves. It seems likely that cross-breeding species, thousands of years ago, became genetically frozen in hundreds of different varieties. None of these could breed sexually so were unable to adapt to changing conditions and survival of the fittest has meant that some of them have died out; in Britain 235 microspecies are currently recognised and around 50 of these are found in our area. All Dandelions have in common a basal rosette of leaves, flower stems without

A Dandelion

Hay-rattle

leaves and a single flower head on each stem. The individual petals are yellow on the upper side and various colours on the lower side, often crimson or grey. The sandy places along the north coast have some rather special microspecies related to Arctic Dandelions.

Hay-rattle (*Rhinanthus minor*) gets its name because when the seeds are ripe they rattle in the seed pod. The flower is generally yellow and two-lipped with perhaps brown or red patches, but it is a rather variable species. The stem is sturdy and has opposite pairs of leaves. The plant is partly parasitic on the grasses around it, weakening them and restricting their growth.

Ribwort Plantain (*Plantago lanceolata*) has dull-brown flowers showing white pollen. There is a substantial rosette of lance-shaped green leaves which have five ribs along them. It is very common

Ribwort Plantain in a meadow

in grassland. The juice is effective in stopping bleeding, well known in the old Scots tradition.

Lady's Mantle (*Alchemilla* species) is a group of species common in the area but not easy to distinguish. They all have tiny green or yellow flowers. The most frequent at lower altitudes is the **Hairless Lady's Mantle** (*Alchemilla glabra*) which has large light-green leaves (70 mm diameter) with about seven rounded lobes around the leaf. The leaves, leaf stems and flower stems are hairless. The **Southern Lady's Mantle** (*Alchemilla filicaulis*) has mid-green leaves about 25 mm diameter with nine rounded lobes cut less than halfway into the leaf. The hairiness is greatly variable. The **Alpine Lady's Mantle** (*Alchemilla alpina*) occurs in high meadows and stony plateaux and has mid-green leaves about 25 mm diameter with about five rounded lobes cut more than halfway through the leaf. Also, beware of finding the garden escapee *Alchemilla mollis* which has large leaves and bright-yellow flowers; it is not uncommon in the wild.

Wild Thyme (*Thymus polytrichus*) is common on thin dry soil such as that at the base of a rock outcrop. It has small

Lady's Mantle; this one is *Alchemilla glabra*

Alpine Lady's Mantle, with leaves divided to the base

The small flowers of Wild Thyme

Common Mouse-ear

oval leaves with hairs and small, four-petalled pink-purple flowers. It has the smell of thyme but isn't as strongly scented as the Mediterranean thymes used as culinary herbs, which are different species.

Common Mouse-ear (*Cerastium fontanum*) has flowers with five deeply notched white petals. Its hairy, ovate green leaves sprawl amongst the grass. It is very common in grassland and tends to have bigger flowers and less sprawl in the high mountains. The **Sticky Mouse-ear** (*Cerastium glomeratum*) is also common and can be distinguished by the flowers clustering together in groups and being sticky to touch.

Cuckooflower (*Cardamine pratensis*) flowers in May and is also called Mayflower or Lady's Smock. It has lilac flowers and leaves in a basal rosette, each leaf consisting of several (often seven) leaflets. There are a few stem leaves as well, also made up of several leaflets.

Chickweed Wintergreen (*Trientalis europaea*) is neither a chickweed nor a wintergreen. It likes the acid grassland intermediate between grass and heath, though it is sometimes found on a purely peaty substrate. Its single stem is usually 10 cm high with a single star-like white flower at the top. Halfway up the stem there is a whorl of pale-green leaves. It is infrequent in Caithness and on the west

Chickweed Wintergreen

Cuckooflower

coast but common in the centre of our area. It is probably another example of a species that has out-survived the birch woodland of which it was once part.

Heath Speedwell (*Veronica officinalis*) has its bright-blue flowers in a conical spike standing vertically from procumbent leaves. It likes well-drained soil, so is to be found on a tussock or the periphery of a rock or a steeper bank.

125

Heath Speedwell

Silverweed (*Potentilla anserina*) has a yellow flower and silver-backed leaves which are divided up into alternately large and small leaflets. It creeps over bare or sparsely populated ground in grasslands, waysides and seashores.

Red Clover (*Trifolium pratense*) has a tight head of pink-purple flowers and a mid- or dark-green trefoil leaf with a white or pale crescent-shaped mark. It can be native or a bred-and-sown farming variety. It prefers a neutral

Silverweed

Red Clover

The small and delicate Fairy Flax

grassland which it enriches by trapping atmospheric nitrogen in its roots to form nitrate in the soil. We have already described White Clover, which likes a barer habitat with shorter vegetation.

A good indicator of sweeter grassland likely to have more species is the presence of the **Fairy Flax** (*Linum catharticum*). It has delicate five-petalled white flowers on slender stalks and opposite pairs of leaves on the stem. It likes to have some calcium in the soil but will tolerate wet or dry conditions.

Self-heal (*Prunella vulgaris*) is very common in grassland that is not too rank. It likes the ground to be grazed and will invade a lawn that is regularly mowed. It has a tight head of deep purple or violet flowers surrounded by purplish-green oval leaves.

Common Cow-wheat (*Melampyrum pratense*) is frequent in acid grassland and quite often found on drier peaty

Self-heal

Common Cow-wheat

heathland. It is probably a relict from the former oak-birch woodland on the site since that is its common habitat in more southerly parts of Britain. The flowers can be pale- or deep-yellow with perhaps purple markings; they grow in pairs in the angles of the long leaves.

A close relative is the **Red Bartsia** (*Odontites vernus*) which is an annual and in our chilly summers takes until August to flower. Despite its name the flowers are pink and grow in a spike on a purple

Red Bartsia

Harebell

stem. It is scattered in groups on neutral grassland.

On a dry grassy bank the **Harebell** (*Campanula rotundifolia*) might be found, though it is at the northerly edge of its range and more common in the east than the west. This is the 'Bluebell of Scotland' though there is such confusion over the name that we hesitate to use it! Early spring leaves are round and close to

Alpine Bistort

the ground. Later the flowering stem carries narrow linear leaves and the round ones wither.

Also found on a dry grassy bank is the **Alpine Bistort** (*Persicaria vivipara*), which occurs at higher elevations, especially on ground with some mineral richness. It has an interesting flower spike – the top part bears pinky-white flowers, typical of its Bistort family, while the lower part has small purple bulbils which can fall off and reproduce the plant even

Spear Thistle

Creeping Thistle

Marsh Thistle

if the summer is too cool to ripen the seed of the flowers. The stem is just a few centimetres tall, bearing narrow parallel-sided leaves.

There are three common Thistles in the grassland. The **Spear Thistle** (*Cirsium vulgare*) is stout and has purple flowers and spiny stems. The **Creeping Thistle** (*Cirsium arvense*) has lilac flowers and the stems are not spiny – it creeps underground, throwing up stems at intervals. The **Marsh Thistle** (*Cirsium palustre*) has, like the Spear Thistle, purple flowers and spiny stems, but it is a slender plant with finer spines and usually a deep-purplish-green foliage. The Melancholy Thistle is described further in Chapter 4.

Common Knapweed (*Centaurea nigra*) is common on ungrazed grassland where it normally grows in clumps up to 1 m high. The plant has hard spherical buds that open to show purple thistle-like flowers. There are no spines on the soft stems and leaves which make it easy to differentiate from thistles.

Yarrow (*Achillea millefolium*) is also common. Its finely divided leaves are readily recognisable and the daisy-like flowers are a dull white.

Knapweed or Hardheads

Yarrow or Milfoil; note the finely divided leaves

A very common plant in short grass is the **Daisy** (*Bellis perennis*) with its well-known composite flower growing out from a rosette of bright-green leaves. It requires quite good neutral grassland and does not occur normally on peaty soil. So, despite being common and widespread, it can be quite absent from some of our large areas of peatland. Plant surveyors can be driven to despair if they consider that no survey can be complete without finding a Daisy!

Many of the species associated with the machair (see Chapter 2) can occur in natural grassland away from the coast, with the species being more diverse in limestone and other mineral-rich habitats. In particular the Creeping Buttercup, the Meadow Buttercup and the Birdsfoot Trefoil are common, the Field Gentian and the Autumn Gentian are locally common, and many orchids may occur.

At higher elevations the grasslands become less rich in species and then eventually give way to other habitat types because high rainfall and harsh climate favours more acid or stony environments. The slopes of Ben More Assynt and Conival have the richest upland grasslands.

A field of Daisies – it was probably over-grazed in winter

PEATY UPLANDS

The higher rainfall and cooler summer temperatures of the uplands naturally encourage peat formation, so many of our uplands are indeed peat-covered and become a natural extension of the peat-moor habitat. So many of the plants encountered on the lower slopes of the hills are common peat-moor plants. On going higher, new plants will be found.

Arctic Bearberry (*Arctostaphylos alpinus*) is a speciality of the uplands north of Inverness. It is similar to Bearberry but has white flowers from May onwards, black berries and the leaves are wrinkled, dark purplish-green and deciduous. It may be difficult to find in summer if amongst other vegetation, but the new shoots with red leaves in autumn are very distinctive. It occurs usually near or on rocks above 500 m. It also descends to the coast as part of the coastal alpine flora on the north-west and north coasts.

Cloudberry (*Rubus chamaemorus*) throws up the most beautiful white flowers from deep upland peat. The leaves

Arctic Bearberry in wind-pruned Heather

Cloudberry on Morven in Caithness

135

Dwarf Birch on higher-elevation peatland

Fir Clubmoss on higher-elevation peatland

Alpine Meadow-rue is only 4 cm tall

are large and have about seven rounded lobes. The fruit is pink or red, maturing to orange, as a cluster of round berries which is edible and much valued as a delicacy in Scandinavia. It flowers in late May with mature fruits in July.

Dwarf Birch (*Betula nana*) is a tree typically 20 cm tall, though it can reach a span of 1 m in a less exposed place. The leaves are small and neat, being rounded and toothed. It can often be found in deep heather where it is hard to spot, but it grows on open crags and on thinner peat where the heather is not so high.

Fir Clubmoss (*Huperzia selago*) is one of several species of Clubmoss that might be encountered on the peat. They generally look like miniature conifer branches just a few millimetres in diameter.

Alpine Meadow-rue (*Thalictrum alpinum*) is a delicate plant with small crisped and lobed leaves and flowers that are very small except for the stamens which are prominent and give the flower the appearance of a yellow paintbrush. It grows in wet upland situations where there is mineral-rich water flushing from rock, hence it is found on wet ledges, calcareous, thin, peaty marsh and boggy flushes.

Deeper peat can persist right to the top of a mountain but quite often it thins out at higher levels in a gradual transition to a stony habitat.

CLIFFS, CRAGS AND STONY HABITATS

When plants grow in the nooks and crevices of the rocks, the nature of the rock determines the flora. In general the

A tall herb ledge with ferns and Great Wood-rush

limestones, mineral-rich mica schists and some sandstones support a rich flora, while the hard, insoluble granites and moine rocks have a dull flora. Shelter and wetness also play a big part, since the thin layers of soil involved can dry out if exposed.

Cliffs and crags have ledges and crevices that, if well sheltered, will support a tall herb community. This can include trees such as Rowan and Downy Birch since this is an extension of the natural woodland habitat. Globeflower, Water Avens, Primrose and Early Purple Orchid might be present with Alpine Saw-wort, Yellow Mountain Saxifrage, Roseroot and perhaps also the following.

Stone Bramble (*Rubus saxatilis*) has bramble-like flowers which give red berry clusters and the light-green leaves are

Goldenrod

Stone Bramble

borne on creeping stems which are more delicate and flexible than an ordinary bramble.

Goldenrod (*Solidago virgaurea*) can be found on rock outcrops, cliff ledges, small crevices and in dwarf form on open

Pyramidal Bugle

stony plateaux. Its composite flowers are yellow and are placed on a central stem to give a rod-shaped golden terminal to the flower stem.

The **Pyramidal Bugle** (*Ajuga pyramidalis*) is a rare plant that is spread sparsely around our area. It has a cone-shaped outline of round dark-green leaves, with blue-and-white flowers tucked in amongst the leaves. It flowers in mid May and then shrinks to an insignificant brown shape which is hard to find later in the summer. It likes free-draining sunny slopes with thin soil. In Britain most of the sites are north of Inverness. The easiest place to see it is, in May, at the foot of the Mound hill, near Golspie around NH779985.

Bloody Cranesbill (*Geranium sanguineum*) is rare in our area, occurring only at the Mound near Golspie and at Lybster in Caithness near the harbour.

Bloody Cranesbill at Lybster

It has bright, red-purple flowers.

When the crevices on cliffs and outcrops have little soil, the vegetation is less rich and more specialised. The plants are small and compact especially in exposed places. Common plants are Alpine Lady's Mantle, Moss Campion, Roseroot and a few others.

Starry Saxifrage (*Saxifraga stellaris*) has beautiful white petals decorated with two yellow dots and has a prominent pink seedpod and anthers. It is one of the

Starry Saxifrage by a small steep burn

Dwarf Willow in close-up

Mountain Sorrel on a scree slope

commonest and prettiest of the alpines. It likes wet rocks.

Dwarf Willow (*Salix herbacea*) is a tiny Willow shrub some 5 cm high creeping over the surface of a rock in the most exposed places. It has small yellow catkins in late June which add to the attractiveness of the plant.

Higher still, there is usually a summit plateau to our hills, sufficiently level to permit snow to lie for longer, wet enough that nutrients have been mostly washed out, very exposed to wind, cool in summer and cold in winter. It consists of frost-shattered rock fragments, patches of thin peat and bare rock with crevices. The common plants are Heather (dwarfed and wind-pruned), Crowberry, Alpine Lady's Mantle, Moss Campion, a dwarf form of Goldenrod, Arctic Bearberry, Dwarf Willow and often also some of the following species.

Mountain Sorrel (*Oxyria digyna*) has round leaves about 2 cm diameter and an obviously dock- or sorrel-like flower. It creeps vigorously in wet places and will seek out rills and wet crevices by burns and water splashes.

Trailing Azalea (*Loiseleuria procumbens*) is a compact member of

Mountain Azalea; the flowers are tiny – 3 mm across

Dwarf Cornel in a wet hollow

the Rhododendron family no more than 1 cm high with tiny pink flowers which open in June and July. It prefers to root into the thin peat and to trail over rocks and stones.

Dwarf Cornel (*Cornus suecica*) occurs in peaty hollows amongst the summit rocks. It is a few centimetres high with

143

flowers that are tiny, purple and grouped together surrounded by four prominent, creamy-white, petal-like bracts. In Assynt we found it at a much lower level – try the location NC291202 for an easier place to see it.

Cyphel (*Minuartia sedoides*) forms tight, mossy, light-green cushions, on the surface of which are tiny yellow-green flowers. It occurs on several western mountains, mostly on summit plateaux, though also on screes and rocky outcrops.

Mossy Saxifrage (*Saxifraga hypnoides*) has starry white flowers with a yellow centre. The leaves are finely divided, varying from red to green with red stems. The plant can take several forms: it can be thin and straggling on dry bare rock, it can be a compact hummock in a damp soil-filled crevice, or it can have long upright stems when it is competing in a

Cyphel on loose limestone scree

Mossy Saxifrage on eastern coastal rocks

Rock Cinquefoil in its secret location

tall herb community on a shelf. In the west it is on the hills as an element of the upland flora, while on the east coast it is on maritime and inland rocks at sea level. The most convenient place to see it is south of the Mound where it grows on the steep rocks by the roadside at NH7623398367.

A very rare plant worthy of mention is the **Rock Cinquefoil** (*Potentilla rupestris*). Although it is not rare in mainland Europe, the plant has only four sites in Britain: two of these are in Wales and the other two are sites between Golspie and Bonar Bridge. Both North Highland sites are on steep cliffs where the rock has a mineral richness. The plant is about 50 cm tall with leaves consisting of five leaflets. The white flowers are 20 mm diameter on long stems which wave in the wind.

Chapter 6. Waysides and Farmland

Intensive arable farming occurs mainly in the east

WAYSIDES AND VERGES

There is an interesting flora by our roadsides. Most roads were built around 1820 and thereafter changed mainly by being widened and locally straightened. The verges have good drainage because of the engineered drains, so even in areas of the most acid peat the roadside may have some grass. It was common to have sheep grazing along the unfenced road until 20 years ago, when fences began to appear along most roadsides. Thus much of the present roadside is open ground with a post-and-wire fence. The vegetation is similar to that of the surrounding countryside except that it reflects the better local drainage. Where there has been some recent engineering the ground is often sprayed with an alien seed mixture which can yield (usually temporarily) some interesting alien species. Another factor of importance is that in winter the roads are dressed with a mixture of salt and sand to ameliorate the dangers of ice and snow; this has the effect of making the verge salty and it also introduces species from the seashore since that is where the sand originates.

On the main routes there is a seasonal

Cow Parsley

cycle. In late spring the salt-tolerant Scurvygrass produces a line of short white flowers along the roadside, the plants having been imported with the sand for de-icing. In early summer the umbellifer family provides tall, white roadside displays but these are natives of the grasslands which happen to be tolerant of weedkiller and salt, so survive when other plants are eliminated or weakened. The dominant umbellifer is **Cow Parsley** (*Anthriscus sylvestris*) which flowers in early June, has its flowers of pure white in slightly rounded umbels and its leaves are divided into moderately fine divisions. Soon, in late June, Hogweed becomes more noticeable as its more creamy flowers open in flatter umbels and its coarse leaves become prominent. In high summer the verge turns yellow with **Autumn Hawkbit** (*Leontodon autumnalis*) a plant with toothed basal leaves and a yellow dandelion-like flower head on a short (100 mm) flower stalk. It is also salt

Autumn Hawkbit with strongly toothed leaves

Cat's-ear with weakly toothed leaves

tolerant and a natural member of the grassland flora. It is very similar to the **Cat's-ear** (*Hypochaeris radicata*) which is most obviously different in that the basal leaves are not strongly toothed.

In good soil the area behind the immediate road verge is essentially grassland which has been preserved from grazing, mowing and fertilising. It may have a planted hedge – the favourites are Hawthorn and Beech.

Hawthorn (*Crataegus monogyna*) is a slow-growing shrub with sharply pointed twigs. On fertile soil it is a successful, long-living hedging plant and

Hawthorn is the most common hedging plant

Northern Dog Rose is usually this shade of pink

Sherard's Downy Rose hips; note the glandular hairs on the hip stalks

occasional stand-alone shrubs are to be found in the wild. It is planted mainly in the east and south of our area. The flowers are white (sometimes pink) and develop to red berries which are a good food for hedgerow birds.

There are some common inclusions in the hedgerow.

Wild Roses occur in grassy areas, woodland margins and sea coast. They are not easy to identify as species but to make it more difficult, they hybridise to form long-living hybrids and double-cross hybrids. The **Northern Dog Rose** (*Rosa caesia*) is common and a key feature is its short (10 mm) glandless flower stalk. In the south-east of our area the **Common Dog Rose** (*Rosa canina*) with a longer (15 mm) glandless flower stalk is more frequent. **Sherard's Downy Rose** (*Rosa sherardii*) is the more common rose with a flower stalk that is covered with stalked glands, though its close relative, the **Northern Downy Rose** (*Rosa mollis*) is frequent near the coast where its extensive suckering stems extend through light sandy soil. *Rosa sherardii* has blue-green leaves while *Rosa mollis* has soft, hairy leaves that are grey beneath. An easier rose to recognise is the **Burnet Rose** (*Rosa pimpinellifolia*) with small creamy-white flowers, purple hips and an intense fuzz of small prickles and stiff

Burnet Rose is the only Wild Rose with small creamy-white flowers

Gorse by a Highland roadside

Broom by the roadside at Loch Fleet near Dornoch

The prolific flowering of Blackthorn

hairs on its stems. It too stays moderately close to the coast but can be found a few miles inland.

Gorse, also called **Whin** (*Ulex europaeus*) is a very common plant on roadsides and covering areas of marginal grassland. It is not native to the area, being introduced around 1800 as food and shelter for sheep. It quickly got out of hand and is now a nuisance rather than a help to farmers and crofters. Its leaves are reduced to prickles and its flowers of bright yellow are the same shape as those typical of the pea family. It flowers January to June, with its major show in April and May. Observant people will also note the much less common **Western Gorse** (*Ulex gallii*) flowering in October. A cousin whose stems are not prickly is **Broom** (*Cytisus scoparius*). It too has prominent yellow pea flowers which show themselves in June. Its leaves are tiny and quickly fall off, leaving bright-green stems which do the duty of leaves right through the winter.

Blackthorn (*Prunus spinosa*) is a shrub of some beauty when it flowers in May in the south and west. The white starry flowers are followed by the green fruits (called sloes) which turn purple in

153

autumn. The twigs of the current year are sharp and black.

Some herbs of the grasslands and forest margins have adapted particularly well to hedgerows. The **Tufted Vetch** (*Vicia cracca*) forms a scrambling mass typically 1 m high with its purple flowers in a tight one-sided spike. The **Bush Vetch** (*Vicia sepium*) is also common with a similar habit and recognised by its dull purple flowers being in a very loose spike with the individual flowers on stalks.

There is a third bushy, vetchy plant with yellow flowers, the **Meadow Vetchling** (*Lathyrus pratensis*), which is typically a 60 cm-high scrambling mass with a loose spike of flowers.

Several species of Willow-herb occur in verges. The smaller ones are difficult to identify, while the commonest and most showy is the **Rosebay Willow-herb** (*Chamerion angustifolium*) – a plant that has suffered several changes of Latin name. In late summer it puts up tall spikes of red-purple flowers at a time when many other plants are becoming jaded and it adds to the scene later when its long pointed leaves turn wine red combined with straw yellow to give a beautiful display right through to the hard frosts of winter.

The **Moon Daisy**, also known as the **Oxeye Daisy** (*Leucanthemum vulgare*), survives successfully by roadsides though its former habitat in hay meadows has declined because of early mowing and grazing. It is plentiful, lining the roadsides in high summer.

Red Campion (*Silene dioica*) can have flowers of red, pink or white which show in early summer. The leaves are in opposite pairs on a hairy stem. It is common on waysides and seashore turf.

Note the narrow leaflets and tight flower spike of the Tufted Vetch

Rosebay Willow-herb flowering in August

Moon Daisy; the flower head is 4 cm across

Red Campion flowers in June throughout our area

This is the hybrid version of the Hedge Woundwort

Herb-Robert

Hedge Woundwort (*Stachys sylvatica* or *Stachys* x *ambigua*) is frequent in the east but more scattered in the west. It likes damp fertile soil and spreads by underground rhizomes. The species hybridised with Marsh Woundwort, probably a very long time ago, and the ability to spread by rhizomes has allowed the hybrid to persist even if the parents have died out. So the hybrid is now as common as the species in our area, being recognised by its shorter leaf stalks.

Herb-Robert (*Geranium robertianum*) has pink flowers about 1 cm diameter, red or brown stems with straight sections connected at an angle. It scrambles on rocks and stone walls, showing its leaves of five-lobed leaflets. It was once a valuable herbal remedy used for toothache, nosebleeds and as a general tonic. In folklore it is associated with the goblin Robin Goodfellow, though the name is so old it could have arisen from other historic stories.

Ploughed land overcome with Corn Spurrey

FARMS AND CROFTS

The most suitable land has been selected for cultivation and has then been improved over the centuries, so it becomes a good growing medium for invading plants too. As some plants have adapted to the conditions and growing practices of agriculture, a battle takes place in a ploughed field between the superbly adapted invading plants and the technologically armed farmer. In the last

Ragwort grows on farmland and waysides

50 years the farmer has quite literally 'gained a lot of ground' and many species have disappeared. Crofters often have been less vigorous in eliminating weeds and it is sometimes more rewarding for a botanist to seek the weeds of cultivation in crofted ground. Overall, however, the march of economic progress in agriculture is bad news for weeds.

The Creeping Thistle and Spear Thistle do well since their prickles deter grazing. This habitat is also suitable for **Common Ragwort** (*Senecio jacobaea*) with its bright-yellow daisy-type flower, strong stem and scalloped leaves. It is a highly poisonous plant for cattle and horses and such a serious weed that it is one of five weeds identified in the Weeds Act (1959) whereby action must be taken to prevent its spread. In the days before agriculture it was confined to the coasts and did not venture into the woods and scrub that covered the majority of the land. With the coming of agriculture it found new homes on roadside verges and fields of pasture. Animals learn to avoid it in the field, but it is deadly in hay.

The **Broad-leaved Dock** (*Rumex obtusifolius*) has oval leaves, heart-shaped at the base. The flowers are in several

Broad-leaved Dock in a field

ascending spikes of small greenish-pink flowers which bear close examination to see the intricate threefold symmetry.

The **Common Nettle** (*Urtica dioica*) grows in extensive patches in grassy ground, especially where there is a history of high nitrogen. It has small green flowers, male and female on different plants, suspended from the bases of the leaves. The young plants make good soup!

The flowers of the Common Nettle are easily missed below the stinging leaves

Cultivated or disturbed ground has several specialist invaders.

Pineappleweed (*Matricaria discoidea*) has tiny flowers in a conical head, initially green but turning yellow. It smells strongly of pineapple. It originates from South America and was first introduced to Britain in 1871. Now it is very common throughout the north, though it did not arrive until about 1930.

Pineappleweed is very common by farm gates

Ordinary Knotgrass in Britain is replaced on the north and east coasts by the **Northern Knotgrass** (*Polygonum boreale*). It has bigger, broader leaves than ordinary Knotgrass and its flowers are white with bright-pink edging, compared to white or uniform pink in ordinary Knotgrass. The formal identification point is that *Polygonum boreale* has a leaf stalk long enough to hold the leaf well

Northern Knotgrass

clear of the sheath around the stem. It is frequent in potato and turnip fields in Caithness and north Sutherland.

The **Northern Dead-nettle** (*Lamium confertum*) has purple flowers with a hooded top lip and a two-lobed lower

Northern Dead-nettle

Shepherd's Purse has distinctive fruits

Redleg has red stems and distinctive flowers

lip. The leaves are toothed and heart-shaped, and those just below the flowers are stalkless. The green sepals at the base of the flower have long teeth, while other Dead-nettle species have shorter teeth.

Shepherd's Purse (*Capsella bursa-pastoris*) derives its name from the shape of the fruits that quickly follow the somewhat insignificant white flowers. The rosette of basal leaves is distinctive, making the plant recognisable when not in flower. It is common throughout Britain and usually accompanies Pineappleweed around just about every farm gate.

Redleg (*Persicaria maculosa*) has dense spikes of pinky-red flowers on red stems with oval pointed leaves.

Common Chickweed (*Stellaria media*) is one of the most common of field and garden weeds. Its mid-green opposite pairs of oval leaves straggle over the surface and neat flowers with deeply bifid white petals give way to small seeds which readily germinate in the following year. It is an ancient weed and foodstuff, though slightly toxic if uncooked. It has long been used as a medicinal remedy, especially for skin problems.

Goosegrass or **Cleavers** (*Galium aparine*) is a tall member of the bedstraw

Common Chickweed has pretty flowers when examined closely

family. It has tiny white flowers and six leaves in each whorl. The leaves and fruits have tiny hooks. These make the plant a successful climber and also encourage the fruits to cling to passing animals (and humans) so that the plant is successfully spread in fields and hedgerows.

One of the pretty survivors of the agricultural revolution, still to be found in the north, is the **Corn Marigold** (*Chrysanthemum segetum*) which displays its large yellow daisy-like flowers from July onwards in both cultivated fields and for a year or two in the immature

Corn Marigold – a distinctive flower in a ploughed field

Cleavers, or Goosegrass, growing up a roadside wall

grassland sown after cultivation.

Farmers have mixed feelings about their weeds. Good husbandry says that they shouldn't have any, but they can be quite proud of the unusual ones. Walkers and flower-lovers also often have mixed feelings. So we encourage you to take an interest in the weeds of the countryside and regard them as a natural part of it. They are very successful survivors in a difficult habitat.

Chapter 7. The Context

THE SCOPE

The area covered by this book is the northernmost part of the Scottish mainland, covering the counties of Sutherland, Caithness and a small part of Easter Ross. The area is shown in Figure 7.1. These are the northern counties of the administrative region called Highland. The North Highland area has its own distinct identity as regards community activities and tourism.

We have aimed the book at readers who, living in or visiting the area, wish to have a fairly detailed but not comprehensive understanding of North Highland plants. It thus serves as an adequate level of information for a visitor

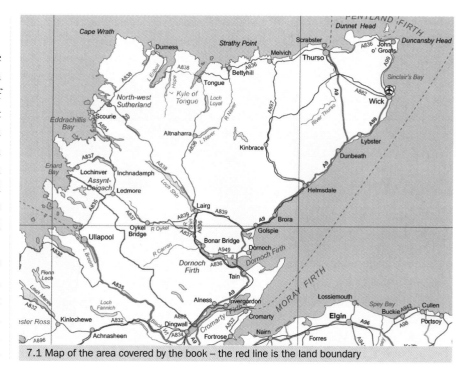

7.1 Map of the area covered by the book – the red line is the land boundary

spending a couple of weeks in the area, or as a basis of a good general knowledge of the plantlife for a resident. For some, we might hope that it starts off a more comprehensive or more specialised interest in the plants. The bibliography will assist further studies. Quantitatively the book deals with 250 species out of around 1,500 species in the area. This has meant making hard choices about what to include. The choice is restricted, with a few exceptions, to vascular plants (that is, those sufficiently complex to have vascular bundles in their main stems, excluding mosses, liverworts, lichens and algae) and amongst the vascular plants we have selected mostly plants with recognisable flowers that are fairly common in their habitat. Occasionally we have described rarities that are of particular local interest. Sedges, rushes, grasses and ferns, while hugely interesting in their own right, have only been included where they add something really useful to the overall description of a habitat.

Each species has a photograph, taken by Ken Crossan, in its habitat and in the area. He has set out to interpret the stunning beauty of the plants while keeping them both in context and identifiable. We have aimed to reveal how wondrous the plants are when examined closely and in detail. We would love to have our readers muddy at the knees through close admiration of plants in the field!

The plants are given English names using the standard names chosen by the Botanical Society of the British Isles. These names are often well known and preferred by the wider public, but they are imprecise and not necessarily understood by those from other countries. For this reason, the Latin name is also provided the first time that a species is mentioned and a brief description is given. Latin names, which notoriously change rather too often, are those selected by Professor Clive Stace in his *New Flora of the British Isles*, referenced in the bibliography.

LOCATIONS AND MAP REFERENCES

The standard system of mapping and locating in the United Kingdom is based on the unique reference grid devised by the Ordnance Survey. It is frequently used in this book and so we describe it in more detail here. The basic grid, which is not exactly in line with north–south or with the World grid, consists of squares 100 km wide. The ones relevant to our area are shown in Figure 7.2. They are labelled with two letters such as NH. Figure 7.3 shows how a smaller square (its sides 10 km wide) can be defined within the bigger square by dividing the big square into ten divisions on each side, quoting the east–west divisions first. Thus the 10 km square shown is NH36 and the tiny (1 km) square within it at the location 45 is the square NH3465. It is possible to define a smaller square within each larger square by the same procedure. For purposes such as locating a building, a field or a walk along a track it is normal to define the location by the 0.1 km square – a six-figure map reference such as NC348652. However, the modern use of Geographical Positioning Systems (GPS) allows locations to be defined to the 1 m square, which is a ten-figure map reference such as NC3482265209. This allows the observer to have a precise location for an individual plant, which is very useful to a botanist!

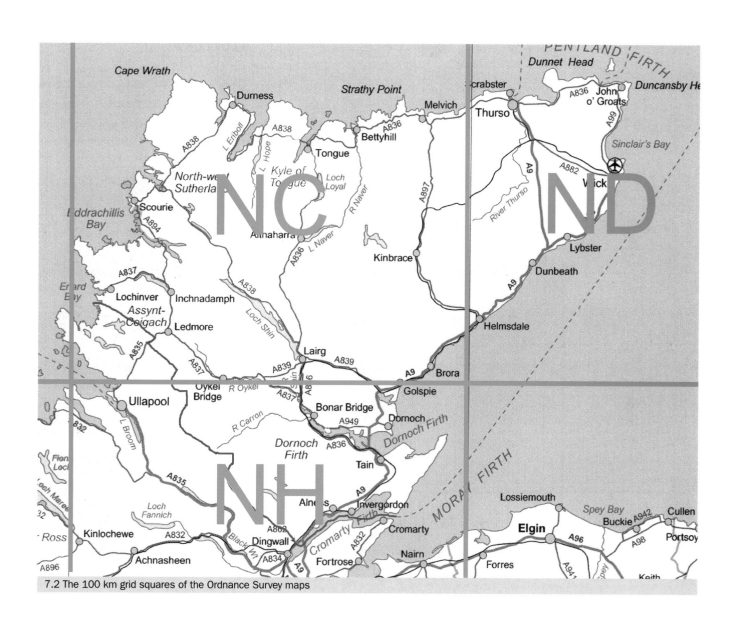

7.2 The 100 km grid squares of the Ordnance Survey maps

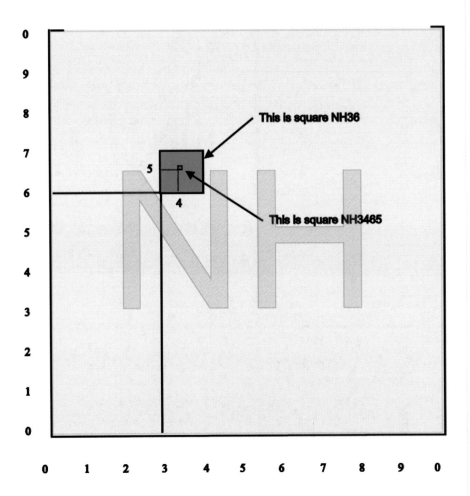

7.3 Explaining how locations are defined in the Ordnance Survey grid system

GEOLOGY

To attempt a comprehensive description of the geology and surface soil across our area would be a large task, so we provide only sufficient detail to allow a broad understanding of the vegetation. In all environments, the principal issue is the amount of soluble minerals in the soil available for plants to take up.

The underlying base rock across the area is Lewisian gneiss laid down between 3,000 million and 1,200 million years ago. Two major metamorphic events occurred involving tectonic and intrusive processes: the first produced the Scourie Complex of 'reworked' gneiss with many intrusive dykes and the second produced the Laxford Complex in which part of the Scourie Complex was further altered. At that time the area was attached to a greater land mass which formed what is now Greenland and north-east Canada.

A very thick accumulation of sandstones and conglomerates then covered the base rock, starting more than 1,000 million years ago but mainly occurring 800 million years ago; these are known as the Torridonian rocks.

They were deposited on land surfaces by rivers and small lakes. To the east of these rocks there were other deposits formed in shallow seas around the same time. But these latter deposits were subsequently metamorphosed into the various gneisses and schists that make up the Moine Succession.

The Scottish rocks began to drift away from the Greenland-and-Canada land mass and the eroded Torridonian rocks were covered by the oceanic deposits of the forming Iapetus Ocean which laid down, 500 million years ago, the quartzites, shales and limestones that are now known as the Cambrian beds.

Between 480 million and 400 million years ago a period of mountain formation and rock folding, known as the Caledonian orogeny, affected the rocks to the east of the Moine Thrust Line, disrupting the Cambrian beds and causing them to metamorphose. The large formations of granite such as the Helmsdale and Rogart intrusions arise from this time. To the west of the Line these beds largely haven't metamorphosed, but they have been pushed westwards in a series of thrust zones, the biggest of which is the Moine Thrust. The era was also subject to much volcanic activity causing the formation of basic dykes and other related features. It was during this era that the major fault along the Great Glen formed; it is a long fault extending from Fort William in the south, through Inverness and on beyond Wick, defining the eastern boundary of our area.

The next major occurrence was the formation of Lake Orcadie, a shallow sea which covered the present Caithness and Orkney 400 to 350 million years ago and laid down fine sediments which became the Old Red sandstone – an area of flat sedimentary rocks.

From 360 million years ago our area was part of a mountain plateau with extensive volcanic activity. Only around Brora and further south-east are there any rocks of the fossil-bearing Jurassic era which created big changes elsewhere.

The solid geology of our area has been formed by these events, combined with the erosion that has exposed these rocks on the land surface. A simplified surface geology map is shown in Figure 7.4.

The last 2 million years have been dominated by a series of ice-age episodes which eroded the rock surface into the now-familiar shapes – rounded hills with corries and U-shaped valleys. The most recent phase of glaciation, which ended about 10,000 years ago, deposited debris from the glaciers on the land. Over most of our area this was a sand-and-gravel deposit, often in thick moraines, which choked drainage channels and diverted rivers. In Caithness this was a deposit of marine clay since the glaciers were moving north-west out of the North Sea and taking the sea bed with them. The melting glaciers also created new valleys to drain off the water and these are recognisable as sharply V-shaped fissures cut through the post-glacial deposits.

The present vegetation began to establish after this last ice age, first with plants such as Crowberry, Juniper and the species we now know as arctic-alpines. These plants migrated in from central Europe and continued to enrich the flora through a series of climatic variations until the last flooding of the English Channel about 8,500 years ago. Plants reaching our area had to migrate across Britain, crossing barriers of inhospitable terrain and perhaps having to wait until suitably mature soils developed from the post-glacial detritus.

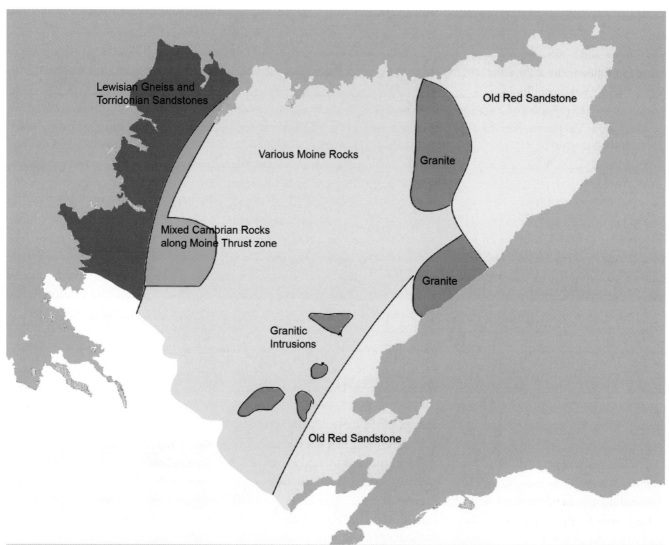

Lewisian Gneiss and
Torridonian Sandstones

Old Red Sandstone

Various Moine Rocks

Granite

Mixed Cambrian Rocks
along Moine Thrust zone

Granite

Granitic
Intrusions

Old Red Sandstone

7.4 A simplified surface geology map of our area

During the last 10,000 years the climate has varied considerably. Pine-birch forest and scrub developed 9,000 years ago followed by a long period of warm and wet conditions which promoted soil development and a richer woodland. About 5,000 years ago the climate became much cooler and led to the extensive formation of peat blankets across our area, peaking in intensity about 2,500 years ago.

Interestingly, in the North Highland area, on the mountain tops and along the coast in the north-west, the arctic-alpine flora of 10,000 years ago has never been overwhelmed and replaced by more recent, more vigorous species. The best place to see this relict flora is at the Invernaver nature reserve at Bettyhill.

The practical outcomes of our geological and ecological history can be summarised by the following points:

- The west coast has ancient rocks of Lewisian gneiss with many volcanic dykes of more recent material intruding. It is an undulating landscape, mostly comprising rocks of low soluble mineral content, poor nutrient-deficient soil and a thin cover of peat. In places this is overlain with Torridonian rocks thick enough to form the isolated dramatic mountains such as Canisp and Suilven

- The long fault line of the Moine Thrust zone gives rise to exposures of Durness limestone, notably at Durness, Inchnadamph and Elphin. It is covered with a thin layer of rich fertile soil which supports grassland and is subject to intensive grazing. Other rock exposures in this zone are of various grits and quartzites

- East of the Moine Thrust zone the rocks comprise metamorphosed Cambrian beds which are exposed on the surface as schists, granites and gneiss. None of these are able to provide large amounts of soluble minerals so the soils are poor or non-existent. Moraines and glacial debris are plentiful and the whole surface has been covered with a blanket of peat, much of which remains. The flora is typical of nutrient-poor acidic conditions except where local patches of better nutrients occur. The surface is mostly undulating plateau cut by glacial drainage channels

- Much of Caithness is covered with Old Red sandstone. It presents a flat surface with groundwater emerging from the fissures. Often the water is mineral-rich. The rock is covered by a thick layer of glacial marine clay which weathers to a rich soil. This soil too was once overlain with peat. In the places where agriculture was successful the land was drained and the peat ploughed in with the clay, but elsewhere the peat cover remains

CLIMATE

In summer the area is uniformly cool. A long-term average of the maximum daily temperature in July is close to 16°C (when corrected to sea level – it is obviously cooler at elevated locations). A useful parameter is that the annual accumulated temperature ranges from 500 to 1,000 degree-days. This is the temperature excess above 6°C accumulated each day. For comparison most of the south of England has 1,500 degree-days so has up to three times the thermal 'driving force' to grow plants and ripen seed.

In winter the temperature is strongly

influenced by the warm sea, so inland temperatures are often much lower than those at the coast. The west and north coasts benefit from the warm oceanic current from the tropical south-west Atlantic (the Gulf Stream) which keeps the coast so mild that palm trees will grow at Tongue and south-west of there. Meanwhile the centre of our area has had frost down to −27°C on occasions. The distribution of average winter temperature is shown in Figure 7.5.

North Scotland protrudes into the Atlantic Ocean and so receives a substantial quantity of rain. This is particularly true of the west coast which has a much higher rainfall than the east. Figure 7.6 shows the distribution of annual rainfall. The growth of plants is of course sensitive to rainfall, but the effects are subtle. It is more useful to look at the combination of rain and warmth: groundwater evaporates according to warmth and the differential effect of rain and evaporation is called the potential water deficit, the distribution of which is shown in Figure 7.7. This reveals that on the west coast there is virtually no deficit, which means that the groundwater level will be resupplied with ease throughout the year, while on the east coast the groundwater level will fall in summer and rise in winter. Another way to regard the importance of the rainfall is to try to find a measure of oceanicity. The word is intended to reflect the rainfall, the humidity, the cloudiness and the coolness that arises from the nearby presence of the ocean. Several complex parameters have been proposed to describe or represent the effect, but we have chosen a simple one, which is the range of average monthly temperatures. By observing the differences between the average temperatures month by month, the typical temperature range over the year is calculated. Oceanicity reduces this range, since it induces warm winters and cool summers – a low range, therefore, indicates a high oceanicity. Figure 7.8 illustrates the distribution of oceanicity, showing high oceanicity in dark blue and low oceanicity in red. The lowest range is 8°C around Cape Wrath and around Wick.

HISTORY OF THE LAND
Early Peoples

There is little evidence of significant population of the area before Neolithic times, around 5,000 years ago. After that there were sufficient people to have some impact on the natural vegetation; this impact would increase with the advance in population and technology. There is little real understanding of where the people lived. It is clear that the peaty and hilly areas had few people. There is some evidence that land of low but positive fertility was populated in the Neolithic and Bronze Ages, but the coastal and high fertility land has been so much used and modified that evidence of early use has been largely eradicated. Also the deposition of peat around 5,000 to 2,500 years ago has covered some evidence of prior land use. These early peoples would have been mostly static herders and farmers.

Vikings

Around AD 875 the Vikings invaded the area, especially Caithness and east Sutherland. They were farmers and travellers so they changed the agricultural practices and probably introduced new plants. Judging by the place names, they set the pattern of farmland use. Words ending in '–bster', for example, indicate a

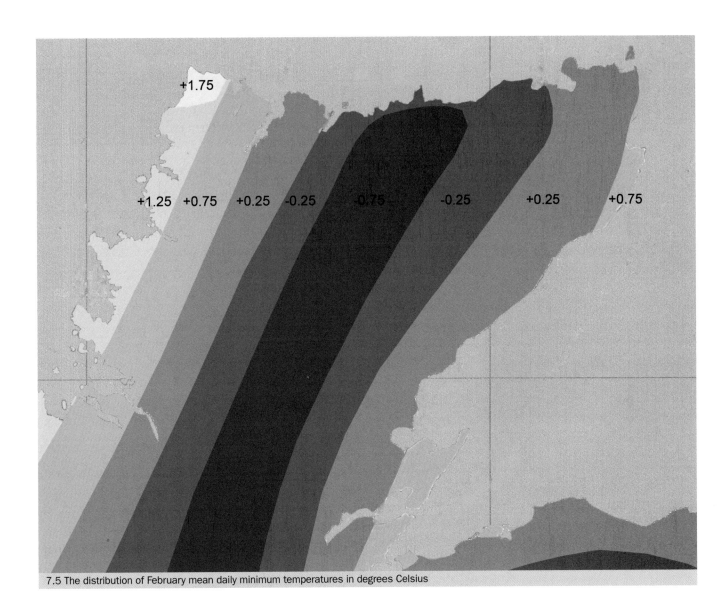

7.5 The distribution of February mean daily minimum temperatures in degrees Celsius

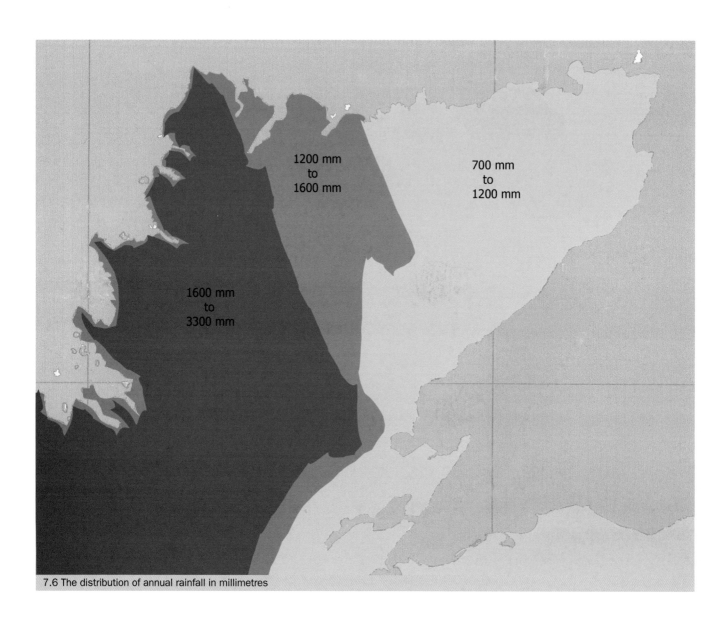

1200 mm
to
1600 mm

700 mm
to
1200 mm

1600 mm
to
3300 mm

7.6 The distribution of annual rainfall in millimetres

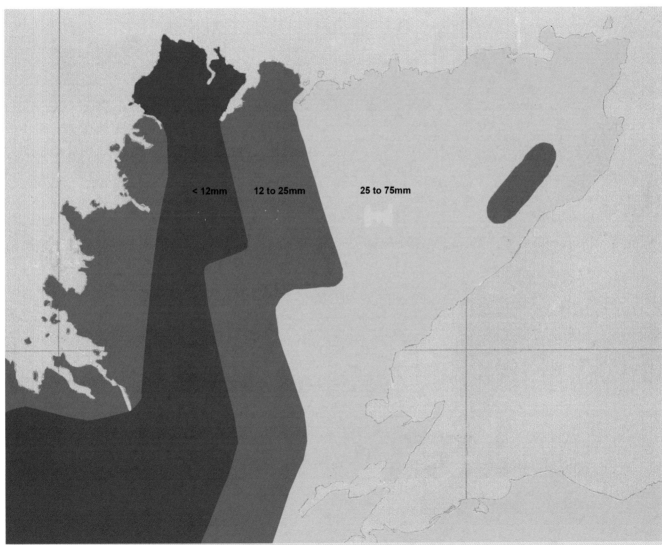

< 12mm   12 to 25mm   25 to 75mm

7.7 The potential water deficit (in mm of rainfall) is the net effect of rainfall and evaporation

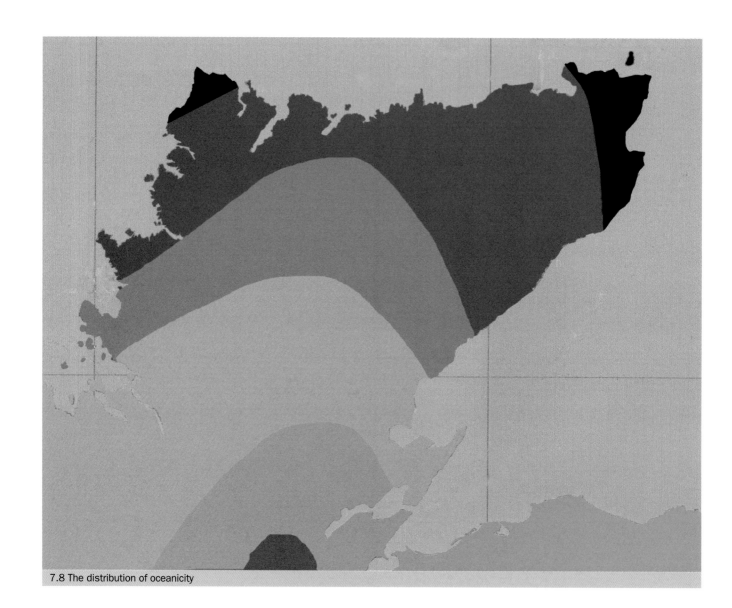

7.8 The distribution of oceanicity

main farm site. Many Caithness farms still have this ending and are thought to have been continuously occupied since Viking times. Also, until 1750 the dominant type of farm building in Caithness was a long-house of the Viking type – indeed many such long-houses survive today. There is evidence of Viking presence in the straths and coastal areas of the western parts of our area – for example the horse-breeding community at Rossal in north-west Sutherland – but evidence also of more ancient forms of agriculture typified by the black-house village.

Agricultural Practices

Until around 1750 agriculture was based on what could be done with the land that nature had provided. There was small-scale crop production on land that was ploughable with simple tools and there was animal grazing on the remainder. In summer entire families would migrate to the more inhospitable higher ground to live in shielings so that their animals got the benefit of summer grazings. The raising and export of black cattle was an important use of the land.

Between 1750 and 1850 there were major changes. 'Town farms' brought large-scale initiatives in which the land was enclosed and drained to improve crop production. Cottars and small farmers were moved off both common land and fertile parks and large sheep flocks were introduced to the hill land. New crops such as turnips were introduced, and crop rotation and fertilisation with guano and lime made a big difference to harvest success.

Beyond 1850 agriculture became more stable, but a major new industry sprang up to create sporting estates. This involved the regular burning of peatland to control heather growth, further drainage schemes and the elimination of predator animals to maximise deer and grouse populations. This had a big impact on trees and shrubs on the peatlands and on the diversity of plants.

From 1850 to 2000 farmers and sporting estate managers had increasing control over the land – their focus on productivity was generally at the expense of biodiversity. Drainage of marginal ground has reduced wetland areas, hill drainage has dried out peat bogs and the

planting of conifer trees has taken large areas of ground out of any normal biological activity, causing the blanket death of the vegetation beneath.

Since 1950 there have been quite significant changes to grazing regimes in response to agricultural subsidy schemes and also a general policy of increased enclosure. This produces very noticeable changes to the plant populations year by year in which there are gains and losses in the diversity of plants. Overall this has a detrimental effect. Plants can only react slowly to changes in habitat and each rapid change produces casualties. There may be new opportunist plant species that get a short-term benefit, but the long-term residents suffer.

In very recent times there has been a stronger emphasis on biodiversity and farmers have been encouraged to take account of the natural features of the land they are working. This is an evolving situation and it raises hope of a better outlook for the plant kingdom.

THE STATE OF THE LAND TODAY

High mountain areas are relatively

unaffected by man's activities and reflect the climatic and geological history. Compared to mainland European mountains, those in the North Highlands are species-poor mainly because of geographic isolation.

High moors and peatlands should naturally have more tree and shrub cover but this is suppressed by controlled burning and deer grazing, so again the land is species-poor. In many places the seed bank in the ground is depleted, so it takes a long time to recover even when the burning and grazing is reduced.

North Highland river valleys would naturally be heavily wooded. There are a few examples, such as the Armadale Burn, Dunbeath Valley, Golspie Big Burn and Latheronwheel Burn, which have retained or recovered a good part of what they should have, but most valleys have been cleared for agriculture.

Many patches of natural grassland have also retained or recovered their character. This is largely because agricultural grazing is compatible with the biodiversity of the grassland in the area, even where there has been over-grazing.

The same is true of coastal grassland and machair. In the west, the ploughing of the machair has changed its character and recovery is slow, but in the east the ground has mainly been used for grazing (since there is better ground available for cultivation) and good, species-rich grassland survives.

Sandy coastal beaches lay relatively undisturbed until the last 80 years, when the rise in leisure and car use made the beaches more attractive. There has been much loss of specialist beach species such as the Oyster Plant in living memory due to disturbance of the habitat.

Caithness and Easter Ross, in particular, had good fertile ground that originally would have been densely wooded. The area was so attractive to early settlers and then to agriculturalists that this ground has totally altered in character and is now man-made farming land, bearing the evidence of many generations of diverse land use.

Acknowledgements

Sheila Butler has been Ken's sharp-eyed companion in the field and many finds are due to her acute observation. Isabell Crossan was a great support throughout the project, providing ideas for layout and patiently tolerating an obsessive photographer. Pat and Ian Evans helped with photo locations in the west and Morven Murray helped with photo locations in the south. Norrie Russell helped with peatland plant photo locations and we are very grateful that he found the only Bog Cranberry flower existing in the north of Scotland in the dreadfully cool summer of 2007! Dr Heather McHaffie of the Royal Botanic Garden Edinburgh kindly read the text for botanical accuracy and made very helpful comments. The book would not have been written but for the insistence and enthusiasm of Lord Robert Maclennan of Rogart.

The North Highland Initiative has provided some financial support to this publication.

Bibliography

Blamey, M., Fitter, R., and Fitter, A., *Wild Flowers of Britain and Ireland*, A. & C. Black, London 2003

Burnett, J.H., ed., *The Vegetation of Scotland*, Oliver & Boyd 1964

Crampton, C.B., *The Vegetation of Caithness considered in Relation to the Geology*, Committee for the Survey and Study of British Vegetation, 1911

Dandy, J.E., *Watsonian Vice-Counties of Great Britain*, The Ray Society, London 1969

Duncan, U.K., *Flora of East Ross-shire*, Botanical Society of Edinburgh, Edinburgh 1980

Evans, P.A., Evans, I.M. and Rothero, G.P., *Flora of Assynt*, privately published, Nedd, Sutherland 2002.

Foley, M., and Clarke, S., *Orchids of the British Isles*, Griffin Press 2005

Futty, D.W., and Dry, F.T., *The Soils of the Country around Wick*, The Macaulay Institute for Soil Research 1976

Johnstone, G.S., and Mykura, W., *British Regional Geology: The Northern Highlands of Scotland*, 4th edition, HMSO, London 1989

Kenworthy, J.B., ed., *John Anthony's Flora of Sutherland*, Botanical Society of Edinburgh, Edinburgh 1976

Lindsay, R.A., et al, *The Flow Country – The Peatlands of Caithness and Sutherland*, Nature Conservancy Council, London 1988

Milliken, W., and Bridgewater, S., *Flora Celtica*, Birlinn, Edinburgh 2004

Raven, J., and Walters, M., *Mountain Flowers*, Collins New Naturalist Series No. 33, London 1956

Rose, F., *The Wild Flower Key*, Frederick Warne, London 2006

Stace, C., *New Flora of the British Isles*, 2nd edition, Cambridge Univeristy Press 1997

Stewart, A., Pearman, D.A., and Preston, C.D., *Scarce Plants in Britain*, Joint Nature Conservation Committee 1994

Botanical Society of the British Isles: www.bsbi.org.uk

Index